Business Handbook

A guide designed for start-up entrepreneurs and
Businesses seeking access to capital

Tony Drexel Smith
&
Darrel R. Whitehead, CPA

SUMATICI, INC. ©2011

Business Owner's Handbook, first paperback edition ©2011.

Published and distributed in the United States by:

SUMATICI, Inc.

Editor, Terry Harrison of *TerryWrites!* of La Verne, California. All rights reserved.

ISBN: 978-0-9840365-0-9 Printed in the United States of America by *Copyrite Press* of Alhambra, California.

www.businessownershandbook.com

www.sumatici.com

The Business Owner's Handbook is published by *SUMATICI, Inc.* – a business incubator located in Huntington Beach, California. The Handbook was designed for small business owners seeking to raise capital, perform due-diligence, and find start-up assistance or incubator services. It includes five sections: (1) 125-Steps for launching a company; (2) ABC - Access to Business Capital; (3) Business plan development; (4) Marketing; (5) Working with private and public resources and other business concepts. Written as a manual for easy reference it provides the insight, resources and straight forward guidance that entrepreneurs needs in today's market. SUMATICI, Inc. is a service-oriented company that provides professional-grade business plans and consulting for business start-up, incubation and growth. The acronym is:

Start-Up, Management, Accounting, Tax, Investment, Consulting, Incubator.

SUMATICI is in the process of completing its Registrations®, Trademarks™ and Copyrights©. Where indicated in the *Business Owner's Handbook*, those designations shall be assumed as either applied for, approved, or soon-to-be approved by the government agency that processes such applications. SUMATICI, Inc. is a California "C" Corporation. SUMATICI is a member of the National Business Incubation Association. Due to its function as an incubator company, SUMATICI operates with multiple entities with numerous strategic partners and alliance relationships. SUMATICI does <u>not</u> represent itself as a law firm, accounting firm or a broker/dealer of securities. SUMATICI is a group of business plan writers, start-up specialists, loan packaging specialists, marketers, researchers, business consultants and plan implementers. Any and all legal references or summaries presented in this document should be checked by qualified legal counsel.

DEDICATION

This book is dedicated to entrepreneurs. Small business owners built America into the world's industrial and economic leader for more than 200 years. Our mission is to support and maintain the tradition of America's strength through small business ownership.

Our purpose and dedication is to assist entrepreneurs in their quest to keep America a world leader. This is accomplished by a focus on keeping its citizens employed, selling products and services the market demands, serving the community, paying taxes and leading others with honor, integrity, honesty and loyalty.

We know how difficult it is to do business in today's market. Entrepreneurs are bombarded with road blocks including cash flow management, government red-tape, human resources laws, health care costs, worker's compensation costs, economic conditions, employee benefits, payroll tax, business tax, unemployment tax, training costs, wage law, and unions as well as municipal, county, state and federal regulations that are industry specific.

It is our intention to make the process better understood and easier to manage through this book – dedicated to the leaders of our economy's backbone – small businesses earning up to $50 million in revenue and up to 500 employees.

One goal was to publish the *Handbook* on the tenth anniversary of the tragic events of September 11, 2001 in memory of the fallen Americans, firefighters, police officers, port authority workers, military personnel, and business owners. Therefore, we respectfully submit our *Handbook* on this 11th day of September, 2011.

Tony Drexel Smith & Darrel R. Whitehead, CPA

CONTENTS

INTRODUCTION

We have been there. Owning a business can be incredibly rewarding, fun and challenging and give the owner a feeling of accomplishment by contributing to the community through products, services and the creation of jobs. It can also be quite difficult: employee disputes, lay-offs, depositions, lawsuits, mediations, fund raising and many other things that can keep an owner awake at night. The least of which may be facing three months arrears on the bills - yet somehow, strong-willed entrepreneurs keep going. It seems the biggest hurdle is always the same – a lack of reserves and cash flow.

Darrel and I have worked with clients seeking as little as a $10,000 line of credit and we have represented projects as large as a five-year pro forma for a $305 million dollar manufacturing company and $1.1 billion dollar resort. We have processed SBA loans, venture capital packages and all manner of business finance documents.

Together we have worked with more than 1,000 clients, played major and minor roles in the development of more than 700 business plans and more than 250 business start-ups. We have experienced many success stories. Yet, one of the most difficult aspects of our mission is knowing that not all projects are viable – and it's a challenge telling a client that we believe a project may not work. Business start-ups become an emotional experience for some. We get "it."

Now we are sharing "it" with you. Through this book we will share our experiences including the steps in launching a company; all types of access to business capital; how to develop a winning business plan; define and explain supporting role players such as accountants, attorneys, marketers and human capital experts. We will also show you how to lean on resources available to you such as working with a business incubator, a Certified Development Company (CDC), Small Business Development Centers (SBDC), Service Corps of Retired Executives (SCORE) and other business consulting resources both private and public.

In chapter one, we start by describing the right steps for launching a company. During Desert Shield and Desert Storm in 1990-91 Tony had the honor of serving our country as a Marine in the 3rd Marine Aircraft Wing. He worked with a team led by an incredible leader named Sgt. Ayon. They built air-launched weapons including video guided bombs, laser guided bombs, missiles and rockets. While he learned a lot working with the teams, one of the greatest lessons he learned was to always use a checklist. While the Marines may have been highly trained, the danger of working with weapons required that they always followed a checklist in order to ensure there were no mistakes.

When designing our checklist we considered the same thing – we wanted you to have the most comprehensive list imaginable in order to ensure you know what you need to do. It is important to note that no list is perfect since every business is different and may have nuances we may not have covered. When working with clients we adjust the list from time to time to conform to the specific needs of a company. But, for the most part, chapter one covers the basics for most companies. For existing business owners who may think the handbook is not for them, they may be surprised to find that most of the steps are required to gain access to business capital or prepare a business for sale or valuation.

Chapter one is also the basis of our Confidential Business Assessment (CBA) program in which SUMATICI evaluates businesses to assist in determining readiness, fundability and business plan strengths and weaknesses. While the entire

Business Owner's Handbook is a summary of the CBA process; chapter one is the foundation.

Chapter two focuses on access to capital. In it, we provide descriptions of dozens of ways to raise capital for a company including varying types of equity, debt and royalty financing. With editorial assistance from our contributing expert Matthew Roberson, we start by discussing the owner's personal equity investment options. Then we review dozens of types of borrowing options. Next is a focus on selling part of the company in exchange for investment capital through options such as private funds, public funds and variations of the concepts. Last, we touch on royalty financing in which a company can raise capital through advances returned through top-line royalties over a specific period of time.

Chapter three provides the tools needed to develop a business plan. It is assumed an entrepreneur has experience in his or her chosen field. However, most business owners are not experts in marketing, accounting, research, industry trends, operational planning, staffing or competition. A business plan will identify all facets of the business. It defines the business, identifies the goals and serves as the firm's resume. Simply put, it is the road map from start-up to business success.

As an owner it is equally important to determine the purpose of a business plan and how to best gain access to capital. A business plan should answer many questions. There are three basic premises to consider when developing a plan, starting or financing a company:

1. Readiness
   a. What is the current stage of development?
   b. What are the next steps that should be taken?
   c. How much capital should be invested?

          d. How long will it take to hit the next major milestone?
2. Fundability
          a. What is the best funding route if you are ready to launch?
          b. How to assess funding feasibility, risk tolerance and finance suitability.
          c. What are the capital qualification requirements?
3. Business Plan fundamentals
          a. What has been accomplished and what areas need to be completed?
          b. What are the strengths and weaknesses in the business model?
          c. Have all claims been validated?

Chapter four focuses on marketing including traditional, web-based, social media and mobile media. With assistance from marketing experts Adam Blejski of *Parallel6*, Robert Fukui and Jeff Ray of *High Point Marketing*, and J. Michael Palka of *Winning Spirit Marketing*, we share concepts such as the three aspects of marketing: (1) branding; (2) advertising; and (3) customer acquisition and retention. Every business should have two main parts – marketing and operations. Most often, we find that business owners know their product and industry but have marketing weaknesses. This lack of marketing acumen is exasperated by today's technologies. The two biggest failures in business are traditionally a lack of cash flow and a solid marketing plan. While chapter two focuses on capital, chapter four provides readers a comprehensive summary of what should be included in a real-world marketing plan.

Chapter five is a summary of resources. When Tony started his first restaurant in 1993 he was "green" and didn't have any idea of all the resources available through free, low cost and professional assistance. The *Handbook* provides a list of resources to businesses that are provided by municipalities, counties, states and the federal government. We use the Los Angeles area for some of our examples but almost every community has similar programs that can easily be found.

Chapter five also covers a number of other concepts such as the responsibility for entrepreneurs to serve their community. We also included a list of quotations and books that are recommended for business owners. We have learned that it is important for a business person to stay motivated, keep their mind on positive thinking methods and be in a constant learning mode.

For that reason, we have made it a mission of reading articles and books about successful people and positive entrepreneurial stories to keep abreast of how people "make-it" and to keep our minds focused in the right direction

For example, *As a Man Thinketh* is a literary essay of James Allen, published in 1902. The title is influenced by a verse in the Bible from the Book of Proverbs chapter 23 verse 7, "As a man thinketh in his heart, so is he." In Chapter 5 we outline a series of books we recommend to entrepreneurs to keep their mind focused on success – as Napoleon Hill's famous book's title suggests, "*Think and Grow Rich*."

The glossary of terms and reference section provides entrepreneurs the citations needed in order to improve their knowledge of business ownership.

At the conclusion of selected chapters, we provide a story of working with some of Americas best business owners. By sharing their stories we hope to inspire you.

6

CHAPTER 1
125-Step checklist for launching a business

Inch by Inch, Life's a Cinch. Yard by Yard, it's hard.
~ Jaime Smith - Entrepreneur

The steps were developed in a specific order. However, for existing businesses some steps may be inappropriate, redundant, or not applicable. For some businesses, more steps may be added. However, for all readers, the most beneficial way to read them is a two-phase approach. First, read through them completely. It has been designed to be reviewed in less than an hour. A checklist is sometimes the easiest way to get through a complicated situation. To get the most out of them, follow them by accomplishing one at a time. Starting or expanding an emerging business can be quite overwhelming so focusing on baby steps is crucial to success. One of the greatest failures of entrepreneurs is not surrounding themselves with the right resources and people. In an area where the owner may be weak, he or she should be sure to seek information or hire professionals to help and guide them in that area. That is the point of the 125 Steps: to guide the reader in the right direction and to provide information which may be used to assess the business properly and provide the foundation for writing and implementing a successful business plan.

The next four pages are an outline of the steps written as a checklist which may be printed. To download the checklist, go to www.sumatici.com. Following the checklist is a description of each step to assist in ensuring the reader understands the purposes behind each assignment. Whether a business is based on product or services, home based, traditional or web-based will determine steps to be completed or skipped. This is the basis of the SUMATICI Confidential Business Assessment (CBA). Let's get started:

125-Step checklist for launching a business

- 1 Formulate the business model.
- 2 Determine long range goal.
- 3 Confidential Business Assessments (CBA).
- 4 Draft the first vision statement.
- 5 Take a personal assessment.
- 6 Consider risk tolerance and suitability.
- 7 Budget for predevelopment and incubation.
- 8 Establish financial resources – set a limit.
- 9 Separate personal funds from business.
- 10 Start the business plan with an outline.
- 11 Design and order business cards.
- 12 Begin market research and analysis.
- 13 Research the target market.
- 14 Research direct competition.
- 15 Research indirect competition and models.
- 16 Start the financial model.
- 17 Develop the break-even model.
- 18 Initiate interviews with free resources.
- 19 Initiate interviews with paid consultants.
- 20 Set the stage of development goals.
- 21 Seek strategic partners.
- 22 Make a list of all assumptions.
- 23 Begin due diligence on assumptions.
- 24 Temporary executive office or post box.
- 25 Research trade associations.
- 26 Join industry associations.
- 27 Conduct industry research.
- 28 Hire preferred consultants.
- 29 List all revenue sources.
- 30 Describe revenue sources in detail.
- 31 List direct costs of each revenue source.

- 32 List final non-recurring capital expenses.
- 33 List each recurring expense for overhead.
- 34 Build a time-line for the start-up.
- 35 Choose the business name and reserve it.
- 36 Buy online domain name.
- 37 Order DBA–"Doing Business As" filings.
- 38 Order email addresses–update card.
- 39 Learn the laws about doing business.
- 40 Interview business lawyers and choose one.
- 41 Interview registered agents and appoint one.
- 42 Hold a formal company founders meeting.
- 43 Choose the business entity and file it.
- 44 Assign officers and directors.
- 45 Complete internal corporate documents.
- 46 Interview accountants and choose one.
- 47 Start bookkeeping records.
- 48 Choose tax year and accounting method.
- 49 Apply for Federal Tax Identification.
- 50 Apply for state employer identification.
- 51 Interview business bankers and select one.
- 52 Open a business bank account.
- 53 Apply for a business credit card.
- 54 First draft of business plan completed.
- 55 Define the exit strategy.
- 56 City, county, state and federal agency list.
- 57 Apply for major licenses and permits.
- 58 Apply for capital (debt or equity).
- 59 Develop 12-24 month cash flow forecast.
- 60 Hire business coach or incubator.
- 61 Develop the sales cycle.
- 62 Develop prototypes.
- 63 Develop a specific customer list.
- 64 Start test markets.

- 65 Track test market data.
- 66 Interview intellectual property lawyers.
- 67 File for intellectual property protection.
- 68 Start management and operations plan.
- 69 Create a PowerPoint about the Company.
- 70 Interview manufactures and vendors.
- 71 Define ethics and community program.
- 72 Interview real estate agents and hire one.
- 73 Research cities for operations.
- 74 Investigate zoning and entitlements.
- 75 Review all location options.
- 76 Contact utility companies.
- 77 Choose business headquarters - execute.
- 78 Interview website developers and choose one.
- 79 Interview Insurance companies.
- 80 Purchase all applicable insurance policies.
- 81 Register with State and Federal agencies.
- 82 Turn on all utilities: electric, water and gas.
- 83 Turn on phone, media and internet.
- 84 Formulate the marketing plan.
- 85 Make contact with potential vendors.
- 86 Design a company logo.
- 87 Design branding concepts.
- 88 Review public relations considerations.
- 89 Develop the advertising plan.
- 90 Approve the company logo and branding.
- 91 Join the Chamber of Commerce.
- 92 Make contact with potential customers.
- 93 Interview architects and designers.
- 94 Hire a team for building or improvements.
- 95 Apply for building permits.
- 96 Apply for resale permit.
- 97 Apply for a surety bond.

- 98 Build the facility or finish improvements.
- 99 Install fixtures, furniture and equipment.
- 100 Order and install signage.
- 101 Call vendors to order initial inventory.
- 102 Stock the office with necessary supplies.
- 103 Start the staff interview process.
- 104 Interview payroll companies.
- 105 Implement the marketing plan.
- 106 Website live to the public.
- 107 Interview and hire a printing company.
- 108 Implement social media plan.
- 109 Apply for a city business license.
- 110 Select a credit card merchant service.
- 111 Design policies and procedures.
- 112 Start hiring.
- 113 Start training new staff members.
- 114 Host a pre-grand opening event.
- 115 Assess lessons learned.
- 116 Start selling – buy contact manager.
- 117 Start customer retention management.
- 118 Contact local economic partnership.
- 119 Implement operations and marketing.
- 120 Make public announcements.
- 121 Begin regulatory compliance procedures.
- 122 Join peer and networking groups.
- 123 Hold a grand opening event.
- 124 Submit press releases.
- 125 Reset goals, evaluate and adjust.

1 Formulate the business model. According to *Investopedia.com* a business model is, "The plan implemented by a company to generate revenue and make a profit from operations. The model includes the components and functions of the business, as well as the revenues it generates and the expenses it incurs." For simplicity, let's use the example of a restaurant. In creating a model for a restaurant, defining the model requires the following fundamental concepts:

Industry, sector and sub-sector. Restaurants fall in the hospitality industry; the sector is food and beverage; the sub-sectors may be fast food, quick serve, casual dining or fine dining. Each is a variant of the model. Fast food tends to have lower margins but higher volume. Quick serve tends to have low payroll because it does not have servers. Casual dining tends to have good margins and volume as they typically offer alcohol, turn tables in about an hour and if maximized, they do well. Fine dining has higher payroll and food costs but the prices can create high gross margins.

The next thing to tackle is whether to purchase an existing business, buy a franchise or start a restaurant from scratch. With the franchised model the owner pays into a fund for royalties and marketing with the theory that sales will start quickly. A stand alone restaurant may focus its marketing locally and not have the additional overhead of a franchise.

Restaurants tend to differentiate themselves by either focusing on quality food, or great service or exceptional prices. It is rare to find all three. The model should define the balance between the three. Additionally, restaurants tend to require a theme of some kind with a niche that draws traffic and builds customer loyalty because repeat business is the main thrust of a restaurant's success. Another issue for restaurants is capacity. Determining the number of tables and chairs drives the capacity issue by requiring the owner to consider how fast the tables can turn, in how many hours. This drives the size of the staff, price strategy and quality of service and quality of food. While a restaurant may be a simple way of explaining model selection, the process of creating a model is similar for developing any business. This includes defining the industry, sector, sub-sector, capacity, marketing, niche, purchasing or starting and strategy.

While formulating the business model it is also a good idea to begin the organizational process. Create a five-section notebook or create an electronic file on an *iPad* or other similar device which is carried at all times. A business owner never knows when an idea will come to mind. Keep napkins handy too since we all know how many companies start on a napkin in a coffee shop. Separate the sections: (1) section for product/service; (2) section for marketing; (3) section for financial models; (4) section for management and operations; (5) section for additional notes, photos and diagrams.

If the plan is to purchase an existing business, the process is slightly different than starting one. During the process of investigating a business being considered for purchase, contact a business plan writer, business broker, accountant and business attorney. Their professional advice will help make the right decision and avoid legal and financial pitfalls. Unfortunately, many business owners do not reveal all their reasons for selling. Research the business' tax returns, run public reports and obtain their status as a legal business. One way to find out the reasons a business is selling is to ask the employees who work for the current operator. Employees are more likely to tell the whole story.

Check the Secretary of State's website to verify competitor's legal status as a business entity in the state. Once at the homepage, go to the business portal. Once there, go to the search engine and type in their business name.

2 *Determine the strategic plan.* Strategic Planning is a process, not a document nor an end result per 'se. It is time to gather data, analyze, set a course and direction, create and communicate the vision, involve all stakeholders, and starts from bottom up. If there is a need is to develop a 'Business Plan' limit the 'strategic' thinking and planning to those issues necessary to produce a quality 'tactical' plan.

The first consideration is where in the supply chain the company will be serving its customers. Many service-based and all product-based companies have a supply chain. For example, for a company selling to retail markets, the vertical starts with raw material acquisition, then manufacturing, then shipping, then wholesale selling (with or without brokers and agents), then there may be more shipping, distribution and final delivery to the retail store that sells to the end user. In making strategic plans, it is important to determine where the company is on the vertical line and then plan accordingly.

The key is knowing the destination. In the famous novel *Alice's Adventures in Wonderland* (commonly shortened to *Alice in Wonderland*) written in 1865 by English author Charles Lutwidge Dodgson (under the pseudonym Lewis Carroll). The following dialog occurs between Alice and the Cat:

> Alice: *"Would you tell me, please, which way I ought to go from here?"*
> *"That depends a good deal on where you want to get to,"* said the Cat.
> *"I don't much care where--"* said Alice.
> *"Then it doesn't matter which way you go,"* said the Cat.
> *"--so long as I get somewhere,"* Alice added as an explanation.
> *"Oh, you're sure to do that,"* said the Cat, *"if you only walk long enough."*

(The previous quote is often mistakenly referred to as: "If you don't know where you're going, any road will get you there." But this line is not in "Alice in Wonderland".) However, the underlying point is well made.

Strategic Planning helps: (1) establish direction and develop metrics to measure progress; (2) establish strategic goals - targets, milestones etc. are key metrics; (3) communicate to internal and external constituencies (e.g., shareholders, employees, potential investors, customers); (4) sets the appropriate strategic and operational priorities for the company.
Many business people and entrepreneurs spend tremendous resources and accomplish little in their 'strategic planning' process. Everybody likes to 'talk and strategize' – few are 'action oriented'. Strategic thinking is important and the process has merit – but the process needs discipline like all projects.

3 Confidential Business Assessment (CBA). The CBA-Score™ is a web based Confidential Business Analysis Software System known as "CBA." The website describes it this way, "The Confidential Business Analysis Software system provides due diligence for entrepreneurs and investors that helps determine the validity of a business idea primarily for funding." The system is based on a 200-question assessment with varying weighted answers. The service was developed to provide a number of deliverables to customers including an assessment of the business, funding feasibility, and an outline of a business plan. Clients pay a nominal fee online, complete the evaluation, and receive the assessment within five business days.

4 Draft the first mission/vision statement. Writing a draft mission statement will provide clarity and will move the business forward more quickly. When challenged with difficult decisions, it is wise to refer to the original mission statement of the company. When writing a mission statement, be sure to include the basics:

1. Who will buy the product/service(s)?
2. What is the product/service(s)?
3. Why is the product/service(s) superior?
4. When are the product/service(s) provided - if applicable?
5. Where are the geographic boundaries?
6. How are the product/service(s) delivered to the customers?

Here is a sample: "ABC Technologies is a world-wide industry leader in developing mid-sized business accounting software. By targeting $5-$10 million companies, ABC is able to focus staff training, production, marketing, sales and product implementation plans in a consistent and profitable manner."

5 Take a personal assessment. Determine strengths and weaknesses. Be honest about these. Someone may be a talented operator but weak in marketing, or the other way around. Another may have a high-level college education or street smarts. And another person may be great at managing money or time, or neither. The point is, when engaging bankers and investors and potentially launching a company, determine what personal talents are available. Write a resume based on personal experience and education related to the business being considered. Once the resume is finished, think from the perspective of a banker or investor and ask, "Is this person qualified to run this business?"

6 Consider risk tolerance and suitability. Once a solid idea has been developed and put on paper, review it with close allies including a spouse, financial planner, stock broker, and possibly a business consultant. As a business owner it is important to take a personal assessment of the skills needed to be successful.

A key to business success is meeting with a financial planner early in the planning process. It would be foolish to wait until the business is in dire need of money to establish a relationship with a financial planner unfamiliar with the business. The financial planner will help determine the potential business owner's risk tolerance, make a strong evaluation of the business owner's financial position and determine what is needed to make the investment. It is difficult for a financial planner to establish true "risk tolerance" once a business owner is desperate for cash flow.
In addition, by speaking with a financial planner the owner can assess suitability for ownership. A consultant will ensure it is a good idea in terms of marketing and production. A consultant can ensure the potential owner's lifestyle is a good match for the industry. He can also review the realities of the financial impact this will have on the owner and ensure the goals are valid. An entrepreneurial consultant can also investigate specific business models for the best possible fit. Finally, a consultant will help determine whether to create a new business, purchase an existing business or possibly franchise. Throughout this publication there are no-cost and low cost alternatives to hiring an expensive adviser. Use good judgment in choosing advisers. In many instances, seeking multiple opinions is smart. You don't have to be the smartest person, just smart enough to hire the smartest people- Matthew Roberson.

*7 **Budget for predevelopment and incubation.*** If managed properly, the first 56 steps should take 30-90 days with a budget of less than $5,000 to $20,000 with an average expenditure of $15,000. In these first steps the business model should be well defined and not require any long term commitments or expensive capital costs. For some entrepreneurs, this is the best $15,000 investment ever made because nearly half of all the business models we see end up failing. We call it, "pulling the trigger." Once the owner passes step 56, the commitment level and risk goes up significantly. Developing the budget for each phase of the business start-up or expansion is critical. The budget should include costs for research time, prototype creation, consultants, accountants, attorney's fees and any other start-up costs. This will also help to create a timeline that matches the budget.

8 Establish financial resources – set a limit. While an owner may stop at any time up to step 56, going beyond step 57 requires an even higher level of commitment. Every business is different but our average project over the past five years has been $600,000 past step 57. This is a crucial issue – how much cash should be put at risk by the founder and how much may be needed from financial institutions or investors or both? By establishing resources and determining a limit of potential loss in a worst case scenario is vital. We have seen too many divorces, partnership break-ups and all manner of sad situation because a limit was not set early on.

9 Separate personal funds from business. Building on Steps 7 and 8, Step 9 is the physical movement of money and defining the separation of personal and business expenses. This is important for taxes, bookkeeping and banking. This may also include the dedication of a credit card for the business. Since the owner does not yet have all the proper documentation for a business checking account, it may be appropriate to create a separate checking account, albeit opened as a personal account with one's social security number. This will make it easy to set limits of potential loss, separate funds and share the initial cost of predevelopment with the accountants in Step 46. These funds will be converted during Step 52 when opening a business bank account, at which time, the account opened in Step 9 should be closed and records transferred to the company's bookkeeping records. A business account cannot be established without all proper documentation. While the types and requirements for business accounts vary, typically, the minimum documentation includes proof of the establishment of a business entity and the identity of the owners. It is therefore wise to open a separate, personal checking account used temporarily for business checking until the necessary business documentation is in order. This temporary account will provide a record of expenses as well as documentation for an accountant to work with and for tax purposes.

As with banking, it is best not to mix personal and business life on one computer. It is often difficult to write off a personal computer for tax purposes anyway. When purchasing a computer, it's best to contact a computer repair, maintenance or network company. They can help to properly set up the computer for business needs.

10 Start the business plan with an outline. A well-written business plan takes weeks or months to complete. By creating an outline the plan can be filled in as data become available during the following steps. To begin the business plan, take all the information gathered from previous steps in this handbook chapter and place them into an outline. Chapter Three of the *Business Owner's Handbook* is dedicated to the development of a comprehensive plan, so understand that this outline is only a summary. The Business Description defines products or services; The Company profile; Ownership and the current stage of development and/or history. The marketing section should include: (1) Target market; (2) Niche; (3) Branding; (4) Advertising; (5) Customer Retention Management and (6) Competition.

The next section is the pro forma which includes three to five years of sales projections, daily sales worksheets, cash flow plan, balance sheets, and projected profit and loss statements, worksheets explaining the breakdown of the product or service. The next section is for management including a daily operational plan, insurance, management team, Strengths, Weaknesses, Opportunities, and Threats. Next is the supporting documents including photos, maps, floor plans, sampling, test market research and a bibliography.

11 Design and order business cards. Before beginning market research, interviews and introductions it is a good idea to create a business card with initial contact information. In this stage the owner may consider opening a temporary email address through Gmail or Yahoo that uses a proposed business name as the user name. For quite some time I (Tony) used businessfinancedocuments@gmail.com before he launched his company. Business cards designed later in the steps will include the final business name, logos and website information. We have often seen problems arise by handing out business cards from an employer or other business unrelated to the new company, so make a clear distinction here – just a plain card with name, phone and email is all that is needed. Only order 100 cards or less or make them through a printer at the office. These cards will only be used while planning the business so don't order more than needed.

12 Begin market research and analysis. Refer to Steps 1 and 2 – what is the business model and the strategic plan? Start planning for Steps 13, 14 and 15. Decide if the company should focus on Business to Business (B2B), Business to Consumer (B2C) or Business to Government (B2G). This should be the hypothesis stage - begin defining assumptions about the market including its size, demand for the product or service and market penetration possibilities. Consider geography – is this business local or global?

13 Research the target market. Once Step 12 has been completed, make a detailed list of everyone who would buy the product/service(s). Be specific. How many potential buyers are in the market? If selling B2C, what are the demographics of the target market? These include age, income, social links, marital status, education and buying patterns. This information can come from any number of sources both public and private, free and for a fee. One macro source is the U.S. Bureau of Labor Statistics (www.bls.gov). Another government source for data is the U.S. Census Bureau (www.census.gov). For B2B, the best source is likely industry associations. For B2G the best sources are RFP (Request for Proposal) sites that define municipal, county, state and government purchases. There are many other sites available that charge fees for market research such as www.marketresearch.com.

14 Research direct competition. What competition is already serving the target market? This list of competitors should be direct competitors that are marketing to the same clients in the same size market. Research competitors thoroughly – what is their model, sales and budget. Know everything about them. Sometimes it is best to take a look at the largest companies in an industry to set parameters, industry expected financials, target market assumptions and market size. Buy information about competitors when necessary. Use resources such as the following websites that are thorough:
- cityinfo.com;
- infousa.com;
- knowx.com;
- moodys.com;
- dunandbradstreet.com;

- standardandpoors.com;
- superyellowpages.com.

15 Research indirect competition and models. An important aspect of market research is considering how macro and micro economics come into play when defining market size, market share and market penetration models. Often by researching indirect competition the owner can learn more about the market and expand the model. While direct competition tends to focus on apples to apples, indirect considers apples to oranges since they are both a fruit – the same is true for business. For example, if launching a used car business it is important to know the new car business industry statistics as well. By knowing about new cars the company can decide pricing models, commissions and target market data which helps determine the market for comparison, market differentiators and barriers to entry.

16 Start the financial model. Once research about the product and/or service has been established, keep moving forward by developing budgeting worksheets to establish costs. It may be beneficial to hire a professional budgeting specialist or an accountant to assist in this process. The worksheets should establish: how much does the product/service(s) cost to produce; what do the raw materials cost; how much labor is required; what are the price point discounts available?

Cash is always king. The key to any successful business is cash management and any lender/investor will look for how the company proposes to do it. Financial worksheets are the supporting documents that will take all the notes accumulated from steps 1-15 and put them into workable documents. It is easiest to create the worksheets with a computer spreadsheet software program. The worksheets are the basis for the financial statements which will be needed for the financial section of the business plan. The following worksheets should be created (Note: this is a very simplified, basic list.):

- Income generated from the product or service. (The prices to be charged multiplied by the projected number of clients/customers over a specific period of time – normally monthly).
- Cost of doing business worksheets. For example, a restaurant has a cost of doing business in food and liquor. A cost of doing business worksheet for a restaurant would include all the raw foods, ingredients, spices, mixes, vegetables, meats, alcohol, etc. It would not include payroll, rent and overhead costs such as insurance.
- Expenses worksheet (All costs not including making/creating the product). Many refer to this as the "overhead."
- Projected Profit & Loss Statements.
- Cash Flow Management and Analysis.
- Expected Return on Investment (ROI); interest rates on loans; raw material costs and how they may fluctuate.

17 Develop the break-even model. The break-even model defines the moment in time in which sales, cost of goods, overhead, administrative costs, payroll and all other costs match. The formula can be a challenge because some costs are viable while others are fixed. A professional will have no trouble with this calculation.

18 Initiate interviews with free resources. Free resources are highly underutilized. Free advice and counseling is provided by varying levels of government and non-profit organizations. It is best to start with the city and work outward. Free resources are provided in great detail in Chapter Six including the resources available to small business owners such as: City Economic Planning and Development Departments; City Libraries; City Redevelopment Agencies and City Economic Development Councils. The next level is from county, regional, state and federally funded organizations in place to assist businesses. They may include: United States Small Business Administration; Small Business Development Centers; Community Colleges; Internal Revenue Service; Federal Trade Commission (FTC); Securities and Exchange Commission; Department of Commerce; Employment Development Department – Pasadena; State Board of Equalization; Service Corps of Retired Executives (SCORE); Air Quality Management District; Utility Companies; and the Secretary of State in which the business will reside.

Websites to review (with fees and without) include:
- www.moodys.com;
- www.onesource.com;
- www.firstgov.gov;
- www.allbusiness.com;
- www.sba.gov;
- www.business.gov;
- www.smartbiz.com;
- www.hoovers.com;
- www.surveymonkey.com;
- www.ask.com;
- and of course www.google.com and www.yahoo.com.

City and County Libraries: Another source for free information is the library. The public library is a good partner in making a small business a success. County Library systems have invested millions of dollars to provide research materials free of charge. University libraries are amazing resources as well.

19 Initiate interviews with paid consultants. While it may not be time to hire consultants, it is time to start interviewing them. Most professionals will provide a free first meeting for introductions and to establish the need and develop relationships. During the course of such meetings the entrepreneur can not only meet potential partners and consultants, most often the owner will learn more as well. Paid consultants may be business coaches, peer-group organizations and industry experts. Be sure to get their contact information, ask for proposals and make notes summarizing the meetings.

20 Set the stage of development goals. When writing a business plan, it's important to show documentation and dates of progress. Setting stage of development goals is vital to staying on a time and financial budget. Buy a card file, expandable file folder, a mileage logbook and a receipt file to keep a record of everything accomplished and the money spent. When speaking with strategic partners, potential vendors, potential customers, consultants, investors and bankers it important to be able to accurately define the stage of development. Obviously with the use of this step-by-step guide it is in and of itself a stage of development outline. However, there are established benchmarks and milestones that any business should target. They include:
- Definition of the model;
- Business plan completed;
- Purchase of raw materials;
- Design the prototype;
- Test the prototype;
- Rework the prototype;
- Validation of claims through third party sources;
- Intellectual property applications;
- Company launched;

- Employees hired;
- First sales;
- First profitable month.

Stage of development notes should be kept as each step of this directory is completed. Impressive, detailed lists of stages of development are a key component of the business start-up. By keeping track of everything accomplished, repetition is kept to a minimum. All important team members in the project will be kept abreast of the stages of development and no one tries to reinvent a wheel which has already been built. In addition, it makes it easier to build on past trials, good or bad.

Keeping track of the stages of development will be an instrumental aspect to the business plan, and will provide required research for planners, employees, lenders and most importantly, the business owner.

21 Seek strategic partners. This includes collaborators, alliances and partners. Strategic partners are people and companies that have a stake in the success of the business both directly and indirectly. They may be paid by the Company, or in some cases they may earn their income in other ways or indirectly. They may be brokers, sales agents, industry experts, go-betweens, agencies and companies within the vertical distribution line that are not direct competitors. Be sure not to share confidential information with people who may become competitors.

22 Make a list of all assumptions. Review every claim that supports the foundation of the business. List everything from the cost of raw materials to the price being paid for consultants. Assumptions about the product or service, performance claims, profitability, industry trends, availability of customers and strategic partners. In short, if a claim is being made in the business plan, it should be on the list.

23 Begin due diligence on assumptions. Provide a reference or citation to each assumption. When possible, cross reference the information through free research, government information and third party data for fees. This may include engineers, testing companies, universities, professional researchers, internet research companies, primary research and secondary research. Additional research should be done to learn about people who affect the business including vendors, customers, partners, investors, bankers and employees.

24 Temporary executive office or post box. An official business address, even before the permanent business location is established, is an important step. A business address will be needed when registering the business and filing forms and applications for permits and licenses. Because the business address will be posted for public display, lots of marketing material will be mailed to it. So it is a good idea not to use a home address. Use a "virtual office" or P.O. Box instead such as *Corporate Offices of America, Mail Boxes Etc.* and others. It just depends on how much support is needed. An executive suite typically offers short term rental options but can provide all the services a small business owner may need with global access to infrastructure such as phones, fax, computers, offices, conference rooms and other services such as mail pick-up. On the other hand, a start-up company may only need a post office suite. I do not recommend a traditional P.O. Box because many forms and applications do not allow them.

25 Research trade associations. Almost every industry has a trade organization and/or publication(s). To learn more about a specific industry, contact that industry's trade associations directly. Start with internet search engines using key words appropriate for the industry and add words like "association", "international", "national", "group" or "membership." Once trade-appropriate associations have been identified, ask for trade publications, resource materials, membership benefits, symposiums, trade shows, expos and board meeting schedules.

26 Join industry associations. Now that Step 25 has been completed, it is time to join the associations that will provide the most information and research for the least expense. Remember that at this stage of the business it is not as important that the association may provide a lot of services. What is important is that the organization provides industry research available to members on their website, hold expos or conventions and introductions to potential strategic partners, vendors and customers.

27 Conduct industry research. Review micro and macro economics, industry trends and market data. Be sure to include not only the direct vendors and customers but any business subset that may affect the business model.

28 Hire preferred consultants. SUMATICI (Start-Up Management Accounting, Tax, Investment Consulting Incubator) is a business incubator. It provides an opportunity for companies to succeed by introducing them to the foundations of early-stage business success. Darrel Whitehead, a CPA and co-founder has created a business environment and infrastructure conducive for incubator system performance. Tony Smith, SUMATICI co-founder, designed and implemented the Certified Business Plan© concept; a comprehensive, 87-paragraph, nine-chapter, well researched, financially sound business presentation tool created after 17 years of business plan writing experience.

Services include a full-service incubator, production of comprehensive business plans, business research, financial forecasting, marketing analysis and technical writing. SUMATICI has also developed an online screening program that will save thousands of entrepreneur's time and money through its business readiness assessment. Entrepreneurs and investors will find the software invaluable in assessing business fundability risk. SUMATICI also founded and operates a marketing strategy that includes a network which is a scalable growth plan for the company by providing business plan writing templates, resources, speaking engagements, Search Engine Optimization marketing and financial tools in an online forum to entrepreneur's.

29 List all revenue sources. Every source of revenue should be listed individually so that all the marketing, costs and research break down by revenue stream.

30 Describe revenue sources in detail. Now that Step 29 is complete, each source should be well defined to ensure all direct costs are thought through and that the products and services being offered have been described for the business plan and for marketing to customers. This detailed report will become the foundation of the products and services section of the business plan.

31 List direct costs of each revenue source. In a separate report, list all costs including raw materials, broker fees, sales commissions and potential return allowances. This will become the basis for the cost of goods report.

32 List final non-recurring capital expenses. This is a list of every item needed to launch the company that is not going to continue once the company is up and running. This may include property, equipment, training costs, start-up costs, consultants and, most of all, the Steps outlined in the

Handbook. This will become the basis for creating the use of funds report, the loan amount and equity fundraiser. It will likely be updated and changed throughout the development of the business plan. By starting early, the list will be complete and comprehensive. It is better to shoot high than be out of money in the early stages of the business launch.

33 List each recurring expense for overhead. This will become the basis for the fixed and variable expense pro forma. This should include rent, utilities, insurance, marketing, vehicles and all other items not related to the direct variable costs of products and services.

34 Build a time-line for the start-up. For contractors this is a Gantt Chart which defines costs and the time to complete them. For a business start-up a similar chart is necessary. This is important to determine the amount of money needed on specific time lines in order to decide the best way to raise capital and determine the use of it.

35 Choose the business name and reserve it. Due consideration should be given to the Domain and Corporate name. Do not use a business name until it has gone through all the proper legal steps. Find out if the domain name chosen is available, and assure the business name is available. If they are, reserve them. (How to reserve domain names is discussed in Step 36.) This avoids possible issues with a competitor using the same or similar name. Even worse would be finding later that the name chosen is not available because it's been used by another fictitious name filing or on a website domain.

Corporations and Limited Liability Companies are formed at the state level, and there are many similarities among the states. In most states there is a name reservation process that makes sense to use. Give an attorney the name of the proposed organization, and the state will hold the reservation for thirty days. The Secretary of State confirms that the name meets their criteria and will reject names for reasons that sometimes surprise the applicant.

As an example, in California the name chosen for the corporation must not be the same as, or resemble so closely as to tend to deceive, any other registered California Corporation and any reserved names on record, subject to certain exceptions under state law. I once had a certain Bass Vocalist in Los Angeles get rejected because the "Bass" and "Mint" in his corporate name sounded too much like a specific plumbing company in Sacramento. If the Secretary does not ratify the articles, the incorporation process has to start over, increasing the time lag and expense.

Different states have different requirements regarding the use of "Inc." in the name of the company. Again, California, as an example, does not require that corporations have "Inc," as part of their name, but most attorneys recommend it, because there is a presumption that an organization is not incorporated if it is not part of its name.

A winning business name needs to include information about what the business is, does or sells. Chances are good that a new business is not going to become an international brand. It certainly isn't instantly going to become as well known as Nike. So be sure the new business name at least gives potential customers or clients some clues about what the company actually does. That's why so many landscaping businesses have the word "landscaping" in their name, and hair styling businesses that include words such as "salon" or even "hair designs" in their names.

Including information about what the business does in the name also makes it easier for potential customers and/or clients to find the business in phone books and directories (both off and online).

The only exception would be when a business name is a person's name which is being branded for the particular industry (i.e., John's Pizza). While brainstorming names, don't be concerned in the beginning about length or style. Write down everything. Later, go back and choose three to five names and then begin the process of choosing the final name.

A winning business name has to be memorable – but easy to spell. Obviously, potential customers and clients need to be able to remember the business name. But they also need to be able to find it easily if they're looking for it in a phone book, directory or online. So choosing a business name such as "Dormacacyllin" is a bad idea. Unique is good but difficult spellings are a bad idea.

As a rule of thumb, a good business name is generally not longer than 30 letters or more than three words.

A winning business name needs a visual element. What comes to mind when reading "Dormacacyllin"? Anything? Most people don't visualize anything when they read this business name that I invented. But generally we are hard-wired to "see" images when we read or hear language, and incorporating a visual element into a business name can be a powerful aid to customers' memory (and a powerful advertising tool).

A winning business name has to have positive connotation. Many words have both denotation (literal meaning) and connotation (emotional meaning). A word's connotation can be positive, neutral or negative, depending on the emotional associations that people generally make. The classic example is the difference between "Mom" (which has a very positive connotation) and "Mother" (which has a neutral connotation). And that's why they called them "Dad's" cookies, rather than "Father's"! What this means is that when creating a business name, choose words that have the positive connotations desirable to associate with the company – and make sure these connotations are suitable for the business.

If starting a trucking business, for instance, don't give it a weak sounding or negative name, such as "Oak Twig Trucking" or "Puppy Transport". Instead, choose a business name that conveys strength and reliability. A choice such as "Grapevine Pass Trucking" would be much better. Notice how all these names have a strong visual element.

A winning business name has to be fairly short. Once again this is vital because customers and clients need to be able to remember your business's name (and be able to tell other people what it is)! But it's also important for promotional purposes. The business name, for example, should fit well on a business card, look good displayed on a sign or in an ad, and perhaps even a business name that will serve well as a domain name and show up well in searches for an online business. So keep it as short as possible.

And a last tip: think about the colors when choosing a business name. Colors will be an important component of the business logo and other business promotion materials and on the business website and colors have strong emotional associations, too. Red, for instance, is an aggressive color; its fiery elements are associated with speed, excitement and passion while green is a calming color associated with growth, renewal and nature.

For more information on colors and their meanings see *Color Meanings and Colors That Go Together* by Jacci Howard Bear.

Other name selection issues to consider: (1) Initials [How do they look? Some acronyms do not make sense, and some lend themselves to endless (often off-color) humor.] (2) Will it last for generations?

Create at least three winning business names because once a name is chosen, the next step is to register it and the first choice may not be available.

36 Buy online domain name. Typically in today's technology age, it is important to ensure the business name is available online. Even if the business will not have an active website, it is important to at least buy the domain name. It will cost under $30 for the first year. There are a number of steps required for registering a business name, but starting with the domain will partially eliminate many of the future name challenges. Domain names can be registered through a number of sites including:
- register.com;
- yahoo.com;
- godaddy.com;
- and www.solutionshosting.com

37 Order DBA –"Doing Business As" - filings. Once a business entity is established, it must be properly filed. To file for a fictitious name, go to the County Recorder's office. Once the name is filed, it needs to be published. Any local newspaper offers this service. The name must be published for a period of four weeks. Keep a copy of the public print for business records. Note that the law requires every business to file a Fictitious Name Statement when it falls into the following categories:
1. When it is a newly established business or corporation;
2. There has been a change in a partnership which uses a fictitious name;

3. The corporation has moved and has a new address;
4. Five years have passed since the last time the business was registered;
5. A business intends to abandon a business name.

38 Order email addresses–update card. Now that the domain name has been chosen and the DBA has been filed, update the business card with the new information – but be sure to order a limited supply since more cards will be needed once a logo is chosen.

39 Learn the laws about doing business. Research all applicable laws relating to the business. Complete searches about businesses in the same industry. Complete research relating to previous public lawsuits in order to become familiar with challenges. This way, the entrepreneur will be prepared when interviewing attorneys in Step 40. In this way, while interviewing an attorney the focus maybe on contract law, or intellectual property law, litigators or other specialties important to the industry such as environmental law or corporate law.

40 Interview business lawyers and choose one. Refer to Step 39 for details. However, one of the first things to complete with an attorney is to draw up a statement of confidentiality or a Non-Disclosure Agreement (NDA). This will protect ideas and investments. Have every person involved with the project sign the agreement. Generic agreements and statements are available for sale for less than $20 at www.lawdepot.com or www.legalzoom.com.

41 Interview registered agents and appoint one. If the business entity will be in a state other then where the owner's live then a registered agent is required. For example, a California business may opt to register in Nevada. Nevada requires that the Company hire a registered agent in that state. Many people do this for a living so they are not hard to find. Choose one with a high reputation for a reasonable price.

42 Hold a formal company founders meeting. Each person who is considered a founder and who will own stock in the company should be part of the initial founders meeting. During this meeting the company's name, entity, mission and even the budget may be determined. Note that holding this meeting is a major milestone.

43 Choose the business entity and file it. Consult everyone on the team about the business name, as the trade name and entity should be the same name. Get feedback from an attorney, accountant, business plan writer, consultant, family and friends.

The most common business entities are Sole Proprietorship, Limited Liability Company, S-Corporation, C-Corporation, Joint Venture or Partnership. To keep company assets from being confused with personal assets, it is best to file for a business entity using a business name other than a personal name. The exception would be if the business owner's name is in the business name. An attorney and accountant should be consulted in order to determine which business entity to file.

What is a Corporation?

A corporation is a separate and distinct legal entity. This means that a corporation can open a bank account, own property and do business, all under its own name. A corporation is managed by a board of directors, which is responsible for making major business decisions and overseeing the general affairs of the corporation. Like representatives in Congress, directors are elected by the stockholders of the corporation. Officers, who run the day-today operations of the corporation, are appointed by the directors.

The primary advantage of a corporation is that its owners, known as stockholders or shareholders, are not personally liable for the debts and liabilities of the corporation. For example, if a corporation gets sued and is forced into bankruptcy, the owners will not be required to pay the debt with their own money. If the assets of the corporation are not enough to cover the debts, the creditors cannot go after the stockholders, directors or officers of the corporation to recover any shortfall.

The IRS allows for a corporation to be taxed either as a "C corporation" or as an "S corporation."

Differences between a Corporation and a Limited Liability Company (LLC): Limited liability companies are a relatively new type of business entity that combines the personal liability protection of a corporation with the tax benefits and simplicity of a partnership.

Corporation profits are not subject to Social Security and Medicare taxes. Like a sole proprietorship or a partnership, the salaries and profits of an LLC are subject to self-employment taxes, which are normally as high as a combined 15.3%. With a corporation, only salaries (not profits) are subject to such taxes.

Corporations garner greater acceptance. Since limited liability companies are still relatively new, not everyone is familiar with them. In some cases, banks or vendors may be reluctant to extend credit to limited liability companies. Some states restrict the type of business an LLC may conduct.

***Corporations can offer a greater variety of fringe benefits
with fewer taxes.*** Corporations offer a greater variety of
fringe benefit plans than any other business entity. Various
retirements, stock option and employee stock purchase plans
are available only for corporations. Plus, sole proprietors,
partners and employees owning more than 2% of an S
corporation must pay taxes on fringe benefits (such as group-
term life insurance, medical reimbursement plans, medical
insurance premiums and parking). Stockholder-employees of
a C corporation do not have to pay taxes on these benefits.

Corporations lower taxes through income shifting.
Although C corporations are subject to double taxation, they
also offer greater tax flexibility than LLCs. A C corporation
can use income shifting to take advantage of lower income
tax brackets.

To illustrate, let's take an example of a company that earns
$100,000. With a sole proprietorship, a business owner who
is married and filing jointly would be in the 25% income tax
bracket. With a corporation, assume that the business owner
takes $50,000 in salary and leaves $50,000 in the corporation
as corporate profit. The federal corporate tax rate is 15% on
the first $50,000. Furthermore, the business owner is now in
the 15% tax bracket for his or her personal income tax. This
can reduce the overall tax liability by over $8,000.

***Advantages of a limited liability company (LLC) versus a
corporation.*** LLCs have fewer corporate formalities.
Corporations must hold regular meetings of the board of
directors and shareholders and keep written corporate
minutes. Members and managers of an LLC need not hold
regular meetings, which reduce complications and
paperwork.

LLCs have no ownership restrictions. S corporations cannot have more than 100 stockholders. Each stockholder must be an individual who is a U.S. resident or citizen. Also, it is difficult to place shares of an S corporation into a living trust. These restrictions do not apply to LLCs (or C corporations).

LLCs have the ability to deduct operating losses. Members who are active participants in an LLC's business can deduct operating losses against their regular income to the extent permitted by law. While S corporation shareholders can also deduct operating losses, C corporation shareholders cannot.

LLCs have tax flexibility. By default, LLCs are treated as a "pass-through" entity for tax purposes, much like a sole proprietorship or partnership. However, an LLC can also elect to be treated like a corporation for tax purposes, whether as a C corporation or an S corporation.

Forming a Corporation.
A corporation's life begins when the articles of incorporation are filed with the Secretary of State in the state of incorporation. These articles are a short document filed with a state to formally create a corporation. In some states, it is called a "certificate of incorporation" or "certificate of formation". After the articles are certified by the state, Bylaws and First Minutes are drafted. Shares of stock are issued and entered in the ledger. A good tax accountant is invaluable here because they can recommend tax favored structure around retirement plans, medical plans, 1244 stock elections and S corporation elections.

The State's vary a bit in their requirements for the articles; here are the requirements for California:

Corporate Name: When forming a California corporation, for example, the name chosen for the corporation must not be the same as, or resemble so closely as to tend to deceive, any other registered California Corporation and any reserved names on record, subject to certain exceptions under state law.

In general, California does not require a corporate ending such as "Incorporated," "Corporation" or "Inc." (Except for statutory "close corporations).

California state law restricts the use of certain words and phrases in business names.

Formation Requirements in California: When incorporating in California, the corporation's existence begins after the articles of incorporation are filed with the California Secretary of State. California law requires that certain information be included in the articles of incorporation. The following is a summary of those requirements:

- Minimum Number of Incorporators: One or more.
- Eligibility Requirements: None.
- Duties: If initial directors are not named in the articles, those incorporating in California may do whatever is necessary and proper to perfect the organization of the corporation, including the adoption and amendment of bylaws of the corporation and the election of directors and officers.

Listing Requirements: Incorporators are not required to be listed in the articles of incorporation.

Corporate Purpose: California allows a corporation to be formed for any lawful business activity. A specific statement specified by the state must be included. For regular corporations, the statement is:

"The purpose of the corporation is to engage in any lawful act or activity for which a corporation may be organized under the General Corporation Law of California other than the banking business, the trust company business or the practice of a profession permitted to be incorporated by the California Corporations Code."

Director Information:
Minimum Number of Directors: Three or more, subject to the following exceptions:

- before shares are issued, the number may be one or two,
- so long as the corporation has only one shareholder, the number may be one or two
- so long as the corporation has only two shareholders, the number may be two.

Eligibility Requirements: The articles of incorporation or bylaws may prescribe qualifications for directors.
Other Required Listing Information:

- The name and address in this state of the corporation's initial agent for service of process.
- If the corporation is authorized to issue only one class of shares, the total number of shares which the corporation is authorized to issue.
- Additional information regarding share numbers, class designation and rights if the corporation is authorized to issue more than one class of shares.

Optional Provisions: California also permits optional provisions to be integrated into the articles of incorporation for corporations who wish to formalize additional criteria, such as:

- a provision limiting the duration of the corporation's existence to a specified date,
- special qualifications of shareholders,
- the names and addresses of the initial directors,
- a provision eliminating or limiting the liability of a director in certain circumstances and/or

- A provision permitting or making obligatory indemnification of an agent for liability in certain circumstances.

Bylaws: California corporations generally have bylaws that are written to manage the business and to conduct the corporation's affairs, so long as the bylaws do not conflict with the articles of incorporation. A California corporation maintains its bylaws at its principal executive office and is not required to file them with the state.

Director Information: The board of directors of a corporation may adopt, amend or repeal bylaws subject to any restrictions in the articles. Bylaws may also be adopted by approval of outstanding shares in compliance with the articles.

NOTE: The Secretary of State maintains a registry of distinguished women and minorities available to serve on corporate boards of directors, which is generally accessible by corporations.

The bylaws must state the number of directors that comprise the Board of Directors; or that the number of directors shall be not less than a stated minimum nor more than a stated maximum (which in no case shall be greater than two times the stated minimum minus one), with the exact number of directors to be fixed, within the limits specified, by approval of the board or the shareholders in the manner provided in the bylaws.

Officer Information: Officers may be either listed in the bylaws or elected by the board in compliance with the bylaws. A corporation shall have a chairman of the board or a president or both, a secretary, a chief financial officer and such other officers with such titles and duties as shall be stated in the bylaws or determined by the board and as may be necessary to enable it to sign instruments and share certificates.

The president, or, if there is no president, the chairman of the board, is the general manager and chief executive officer of the California corporation, unless otherwise provided in the articles or bylaws. Any number of offices may be held by the same person unless the articles or bylaws provide otherwise.

Registered Agent: Every California Corporation must have a registered agent in California -- the person or office designated to receive official state correspondence and notice if the corporation is "served" with a lawsuit.

Eligibility Requirements - The registered agent must either be (1) a natural person residing in the state or (2) a corporation which has been approved to serve as a registered agent in the state.

Professional Corporations: Under California law, a professional corporation is formed in order to render services within a single, state-licensed profession.

The professions which are required to be professional corporations include: Accountants, Acupuncturists, Architects, Chiropractors, Clinical Social Workers, Dentists, Doctors, Lawyers, Marriage, Family and Child Counselors, Nurses, Optometrists, Pharmacists, Physical Therapists, Physicians' Assistants, Psychiatrists, Psychologists, Shorthand reporters and Speech and language pathologists.
Professional corporations may not engage in any other business, and must comply with particular conventions in its choice of corporate name.

Annual Report: An initial statement of officers must be filed with the California Secretary of State within 90 days after filing original articles, and every year thereafter in the applicable filing period. This report must include information on directors and officers, the corporation's general business activity, and additional details for corporations which are traded publicly.

Income Tax Rate: The California state income tax rate is currently 8.84% of net income. The minimum tax is $800, which is waived during the first fiscal year.

S Corporations: S corporation status is recognized by the State of California. A separate state election is not required. However, California S-corporations are still subject to a separate 1.5% S-corporation fee, which is based on the corporation's net income.

Comparison Chart for Discussion Purposes:

The following is an outline of the tax and other aspects of the four major business and tax entities. This is not presumed to be the whole story but just a sketch of the major characteristics and a basis for further discussion.

Please note that a LLC - Limited Liability Company can be taxed as either an "S" Corporation or a partnership, or sole proprietorship depending on how the agreement is drafted. The LLP - Limited Liability Partnership is taxed as a Partnership. There are no separate tax forms for the LLC or LLP.

	Sole Proprietorship	Partnership	"S" Corporation	"C" Corporation
Net operating income	Taxed directly to owner on 1040	Passed through to partners 1040 via form K-1 whether or not distributed	Passed through to shareholders 1040 via form K-1 whether or not distributed	Double tax- once on C Corp., again when paid to shareholder as dividends
Net operating loss	Reduces AGI -Can be carried back 2 years and then forward 5	Passed through to partners 1040 via form K-1 Losses cannot exceed partners basis in Co.	Passed through to shareholders 1040 via form K-1 - Losses cannot exceed partners basis in Corporation	Deductible only against income - Losses can be carried back 2 years and forward 15
Capital gains	Taxed to owner	Passed through to partners 1040 via formK-1	Passed through to shareholders 1040 via form K-1	Gains taxed at regular Corporation rate
Capital losses	Offset against capital gains + $3K per year	Passed through to partners 1040 via form K-1	Passed through to shareholders 1040 via form K-1	Deductible only against Corporation capital gains
Donations to charities	Itemized deduction on 1040	Passed through to partners 1040 via form K-1	Passed through to shareholders 1040 via form K-1	Limited to 10% of Corporation income (adjusted)
Dividends received	Taxed to owner on 1040	Passed through to partners 1040	Passed through to shareholders 1040 via form	Can deduct from income 70% of

		via form K-1	K-1	dividends received
Tax rates	Based on taxable income: 10% to 35%	At partners individuals tax rate: 10% to 35%	At shareholders individuals tax rate	15%-to 50K 25%-50K to 75K 34%-75K to 100K
Fringe benefits	Partially deductible	Not eligible to receive benefits	Greater than 2% owners cannot receive benefits	No restrictions
Retirement plans	Various	Various	Profit sharing or defined contribution plan - no loans	Profit sharing or defined contribution plan - loans allowed
Sale of ownership	Capital gain	May be part CG and part ordinary income	Capital gain	Capital gain
Liquidation	N/A	N/A	Capital gain or loss to shareholder	Double taxation-First at Corporation level, then for shareholder
Alternative minimum tax	26% to 28% ATM	Partnership not subject - preference items passed through	S Corp. not subject - preference items passed through	ATM of 20% at Corporation level
Payroll tax	15.3% SE tax - 50% deductible on page 1 of 1040	Partnership income taxed as SE income on 1040	Undistributed income is not subject to payroll taxes	Corporation and each employee pay 7.65% of FICA wages
Items affecting the	N/A	1. income and gains	1. income and gains increase -	N/A

46

partners' and shareholders' basis in business		increase - losses decrease 2. capital increases - distributions decrease 3. partners share of liabilities increase basis	losses decrease 2. capital increases - distributions decrease 3. loans put into the Co. increase basis - share of liabilities do not	
Cash vs. Accrual	Can use either	Can use either unless inventory is a factor	Can use either unless inventory is a factor	Cannot use cash if receipts are $5 million or more or if inventory is a factor
Splitting of income	N/A	Allocated according to partnership agreement	Allocated according to shares owned	N/A
Tax year	Calendar year	Must use same year as partners	Calendar year, generally	Calendar or fiscal year
Accumulated earnings tax	N/A	N/A	N/A - unless S had previously been a C Corporation	Unreasonable earnings above $250K ($150K for PSC) are hit with 39.6% special tax
Excessive compensation	N/A	N/A	N/A	If deemed excessive - becomes non-deductible dividend
Disallowed personal expenses	Individual tax rate	Partner pays individual tax rate	Shareholder pays individual tax rate	Double taxation - first at Co. level

				then at shareholder level
Personal Holding Co.	N/A	N/A	N/A	Subject to 39.6% tax rate

Other Considerations

Ease and cost of formation	No special actions	No special actions - just written partnership agreement	Initial legal costs of $500 to $1,000 or $400 to $600 if you do it yourself	Same as S Corporation
Period of existence	Discretion of owner	Termination if partners agree or on partners death or retirement	Continues until dissolution - not affected by sale of shares	Same as S Corporation with no restriction on eligibility of shareholders
Continuing costs	Minimal	Annual Federal and State partnership returns	Annual Federal and State Corporation returns & annual state filing fee & minimum tax	Annual Federal and State Corporation returns & annual state filing fee & minimum tax
Owners' exposure to business debts	Liable for all debts of business	General partners liable for all debts of business	Shareholders liable only for capital contributions and debts that are personally guaranteed	Shareholders liable only for capital contributions and debts that are personally guaranteed
Effect on entity upon withdrawal of taxpayer	None	Dissolution of partnership	After stock is disposed of, Corporation continues	After stock is disposed of, Corporation continues
Transfer of ownership	N/A	New partner requires consent	Easy to do - just transfer stock to	Easy to do - just transfer

48

		of other partners	new owner	stock to new owner
Limitation of ownership	N/A	No limit on number of partners	Limited to 75 eligible shareholders	No limit on number and eligibility of shareholders

Where to incorporate.

Many people choose to incorporate in their home state. However, if a home state has a high corporate income tax or high state fee, and the corporation will not "do business" in the home state, it may be wise to incorporate elsewhere. "Doing business" means more than just selling products or making passive investments in that state. It usually requires occupying an office or otherwise having an active business presence.

Delaware is a popular choice for incorporating because of its history, experience, recognition and pro-business climate. Also, Delaware does not tax out-of-state income. In fact, over half of the companies listed on the New York Stock Exchange are incorporated in Delaware.

Recently, Nevada has also gained popularity due to its pro-business environment and lack of a formal information-sharing agreement with the IRS. Nevada does not have corporate income taxes. Business filings in Delaware and Nevada can typically be performed more quickly than in other states.

Wyoming has also started to gain popularity after passing strong pro-business laws. It also lacks state income tax, and formal information sharing with the IRS.

Keep in mind, if incorporation is somewhere other than a home state, there may be additional fees to pay and additional requirements to meet. We recommend that speaking with an accountant or tax advisor before making a decision.

Corporations and LLC's are required to register as "foreign" in each state where they do business outside of their state of incorporation. For example, a Delaware corporation that has its main business office in Texas must register as a "foreign corporation" with the Texas Secretary of State and must have a registered agent in Delaware.

States are very aggressive and pursue entities that qualify for state taxation. Do not make decisions about state taxability without professional advice from a tax professional.

Review the Tax Considerations and Corporate Set up.
My father used to tell me, never owe the Government money. It was extremely good advice and is the mantra in our corporate culture. Let's review the major tax considerations of the various entities.

C Corporations.
A C corporation is taxed at two levels. This is commonly referred to as double taxation. A C corporation pays a corporate tax on its corporate income (the first tax). Then, the C Corporation distributes profits to stockholders who pay income tax on those dividends (the second tax). C corporations qualify for more types of deductions than do S corporations. Another feature of C corporations is that they pick their fiscal year, as S corporations and LLC's use a calendar year.

For 2010, the C corporation (first level) tax rates are:

Income	Tax Rate
Up to $50,000	15%
From $50,001 to $75,000	25%
From $75,001 to $100,000	34%
From $100,001 to $335,000	39%
From $335,001 to $10,000,000	34%
From $10,000,001 to $15,000,000	35%
From $15,000,001 to $18,333,333	38%
Over $18,333,333	35%

Some states also have a state corporate income tax subject to a minimum. Corporations that anticipate a tax liability of $500 or more must estimate their taxes and make quarterly estimated tax payments. Corporations with employees are required to pay federal (and sometimes state) payroll and unemployment taxes.

S Corporations

One way to avoid the double taxation of a C corporation is to make a special election to be taxed as an S corporation. An S corporation is a corporation that elects to be treated as a pass-through entity (such as a sole proprietorship or partnership) for tax purposes. Since all corporate income is "passed through" directly to the shareholders who include the income on their individual tax returns, S corporations are not subject to double taxation. Moreover, the accounting for an S corporation is generally easier than for a C corporation.

44 *Assign officers and directors*. As a follow-up to Step 42 and 43, officers and directors are appointed by the board of directors. Usually to form a company and open a bank account the minimum filings includes a President, Secretary and Treasurer. Chief executives may be assigned as well, but they are not necessary at this early stage such as Chief Executive Officer, Chief Operating Officer, and Chief Financial Officer and sometimes depending on the size of the company, a Chief Information Officer and Chief Marketing Officer.

45 *Complete internal corporate documents*. The attorney and accountant hired should assist in the creation of the articles of incorporation (filed with the state), operating agreements, policies and procedures and other corporation formation documents. "C" Corps, "S" Corps, LLC's and LLP's have varying documents required to be filed or maintained in the corporate book.

46 *Interview accountants and choose one*. When firms such as *Jackson Hewitt*, charged with "pervasive fraud" against the U.S. Government hit the headlines, leading to the firm entering bankruptcy on May 24, 2011, what can a business owner do to protect him and get good professional advice?

Although the state CPA societies do not endorse the services of their members, they are an excellent place to start looking.

CalCPA (www.calcpa.org/public/referral/findcpa.aspx) has 19 subcategories with IT consulting, languages other than English, and Industries Served accountants. It can be used as a reference to determine names of qualified professionals.

Look up the license at the state Board of Accountancy website. Look for good standing and any disciplinary actions. Select two to three accountants and ask to meet with them.

With any Team member, I am not looking for "good" lawyers, marketing, sales, or consulting people, I am looking for Exceptional People! What does an Exceptional CPA possess?

1. Has a wealth of business experience. Experience with other businesses in the same business sector is even better.
2. Thinks strategically about available business options. They should offer suggestions on how to grow a business next year and not just compile reports from last year.
3. Helps the company execute a tax plan that legitimately allows it to keep more of its earnings. This extends past the taxes that the business pays and includes the income taxes paid by the investors and principals.
4. Are candid and direct in their conversations and communications. It is easy to find an accountant to meekly agree with a client's decisions, but a smart business person wants a CPA firm to tell him when they think he is heading down the wrong road and why.
5. Helps protect the business from embezzlement, fraud and dishonest employees through good financial controls and procedures. They should also help implement internal procedures to more quickly detect any errors or omissions.
6. Provides an objective perspective about business performance. A sales manager may overestimate sales and the operations manager may fail to add in one-time expenses. A business owner needs a clear and accurate picture to make informed decisions.

7. Saves money and increase profits by helping identify "best" practices. This is where their experience gives them actionable insight into the business.
8. Is involved in the business community. They should have contacts that can help grow the business and form strategic alliances.
9. Have exceptional IT (Information Technology) savvy, experience and support.

How to Interview an Accountant.

"An Accountant, Someone who solves a problem you did not know you had in a way you do not understand....." - Author unknown.

Contrary to popular belief, accountancy expands far beyond taxes. An individual or business owner should engage the services of a CPA based upon his company's specific needs as matched with the expertise of the CPA. With the proper match, a CPA can serve as a valuable resource. The following items can serve as a starting point in the process of engaging a CPA to assist with individual or business matters.

- What are the needs? Seek a CPA who meets them. A new business needs an accountant who is familiar with business startups, financing and business taxes. Consider questions to determine how strong of an IT (Information Technology) department and can provide management consulting.
- Ask for referrals. Once needs are know, seek out referrals from others from trusted sources. Ask friends, business associates, and other professionals. However, proceed with caution. Just because someone knows of a quality CPA, it does not mean that the he is the proper fit for a particular type of business.

- Ask questions. When a few CPAs are found that appear to match the identified needs, start asking questions. Make a list of the matters that are important to the success of the start-up. Such questions can address education, experience, specialties, and management knowledge and business philosophy. As a business owner, seek out examples from the CPA as to how he has assisted others who have similar business circumstances. The CPA should provide such examples in general terms. He shouldn't reveal specific client transactions or other confidential data.

The 5 Keys to Finding the Right CPA

1. Reputation - Good news travels quickly. Bad news is currently the only man-made invention that can break the time barrier. When considering an accountant, ask other business owners, lawyers and even the local IRS agent whom they would recommend. The fact is, ask enough people and a few good choices will appear. We found our lawyer this way. We asked around town and all four of the people we asked referred the same woman. No contest. And they were right; she has been a true asset to our company.

Once a list is ready to work from, let the interviews begin. Don't be afraid to take their time. If they aren't willing to talk now, they probably will never provide the time in the future.

2. Communication – An accountant should never be the lone gunman. He is part of a team. They protect assets and provide the knowledge needed to make smart business decisions. If a business owner doesn't understand what they are doing, and they can't explain it to him, he should run like hell. There is no easier way to get in a whole lot of trouble than to allow someone to play with a business' money without supervision.

A business owner should start by finding an accountant who has the people skills to match his level of understanding. If an entrepreneur has virtually no bookkeeping experience, make sure the accountant team can explain what they are doing in layman's terms. Even better, the owner should find someone willing to teach a little as they work together over time.

3. Guidance - An accountant is different from a bookkeeper. An accountant should offer much more than just pushing numbers around into new formations. They will help guide the business from a financial perspective. Tax planning, how much owner compensation should be budgeted, how to handle contractors vs. employees and a lot more. Pay the money for their advice, it's usually worth it.

When interviewing accountants, ask their perspective on business topics relevant to the industry. Ask if they have worked with freelancers before. Make sure they are familiar with the common perils and follies of the particular business type. Make sure they are familiar with the tax laws that will impact the company.

4. Availability - Make sure they are available to talk when needed. If an entrepreneur has to wait a week each time he has a question, it will directly affect the performance of his business. Ask what their turnaround time is after a phone call. How quickly can they usually fit a client in for a face-to-face meeting? How prompt are they with email?

Our current accountant is phenomenal in all aspects except this one. He's tough to get a hold of and it frustrates me. Frankly, it will probably be the death of our working relationship some day. For the time being though, he provides solid guidance and has been there each and every time we've needed him.

5. *Protection* - One of the major roles a CPA will play is to provide guidance during an IRS audit. Find out the level of experience the accountant has in working with the IRS. This is very important, as I'm told that the audit process is often grueling and expensive. Our current accountant was an auditor for the IRS for over a decade.

50 Questions to Ask while Interviewing an Accountant
1. What licenses do you have?
2. How long have you been in accounting?
3. How long have you run your own accounting business?
4. Who are your other clients?
5. How do you calculate your fees?
6. Do you have any specialties?
7. Do you have experience with freelance independent contractors?
8. How many accountants are in the firm?
9. Have you ever been convicted of a crime?
10. Can I see the results of your accounting firm's peer review report? (Normally done every three years.)
11. Do you consider yourself to be tech-savvy?
12. Are you active in the local business community?
13. Do you outsource any of your work? Do you perform the work personally? If not, what is the review process?
14. Will the person I deal with change? Will I get a regular person to discuss my finances with?
15. Are your services standardized (packages) or do you offer customized services based upon my business needs?

16. Can you help me with 1099's and dealing with subcontractors?
17. Can you help me set up a good balance sheet and income statement?
18. How do you feel about teaching your clients about finance?
19. What was the last accounting workshop you attended about? How often do you attend continuing education?
20. Can I write off my new *iPhone*? (probably) How about my business suit? (Only if it qualifies as a uniform – has to have branding etc…)
21. How long from when I call can I usually get an appointment to see you in person?
22. Can I call you when I have a question? Do you answer questions by email?
23. Do you have the knowledge and experience to handle my tax situation?
24. Have you ever worked with a home-based business?
25. What new changes in the tax laws will affect me this year?
26. What type of retirement accounts are available to me? How would you recommend I use them to my advantage?
27. How will you help me maximize my tax savings? How do you double-check that?
28. How long, approximately, will it take to finish my taxes?
29. Who is your target client?
30. What do you love most about what you do?
31. What's your privacy policy? Will you share my information with any third-parties?
32. Based on your experience, what form of business structure should I have?
33. What do you think of *Turbo Tax*?
34. What makes a good accountant in your opinion?

35. Do you know how to use _____ (your preferred accounting software)? In your opinion, is this the right software for my business? Why?
36. What happens if I get audited?
37. Have you ever been the accountant to someone being audited?
38. Do you personally know the local IRS auditors?
39. What are some of the common problems you've worked through with other companies in my business industry?
40. What specific deductions apply to me (childcare tax credits, educational credits…)?
41. Have you ever worked directly with a client's financial planner? What issues did that cause, if any?
42. What are some of the things I need to be aware of as my business grows?
43. How does your firm handle setting up and guiding me through estimated tax payment?
44. What is the difference between a good accountant and a bad accountant?
45. Do you do your own accounting?
46. Without giving specific personal details, what is one of the biggest messes you have encountered and how were you able to help?
47. Do you provide bookkeeping? Payroll? What other services do you offer?
48. What records should I keep and how do you recommend I organize them?
49. Why should I use you?
50. Is there a question I should have asked that I didn't?

Assess communication and comfort level with the professional.

Once confidence is established that the CPA is appropriate for the business owner's specific circumstances, the owner should assess how well the CPA communicates and evaluate the comfort level with him. How does he communicate? Is it high-level mumbo jumbo, technical talk, or does he laid things out in an organized understandable format? Does he prefer email, phone or in-person meetings? One way to gauge his communication skills is by the manner in which he responds to questions. Is he irritated and short? Or is he professional and enthusiastic about having a potential client? If he's irritable now, just think how he's going to be to work with later.

Don't be concerned with location. Location may be important for selecting a house; however, location should not serve as a criterion for selecting a CPA. The office of a CPA is a not a barber shop to come chat and solve the world's problems. Focusing only on location may mean foregoing the consideration of other selection criteria such as those mentioned above.

A CPA can serve as a valuable resource in the growth and efficient use of financial resources. Seek one who is open and honest about both their qualifications and limitations. Feel confident about engaging a qualified professional who seeks the company's best interests.

47 Start bookkeeping records. Ineffective cash flow management is often the challenge that keeps businesses from growing. It is also the number one reason businesses fail. Good bookkeeping is the best way to combat cash flow challenges. A weekly assessment of receipts, accounts payable and receivables is a vital aspect of running a successful business. Though bookkeeping can be managed by the owner, it is best to hire a full or part-time bookkeeper or an independent contractor. Constant communication with the bookkeeper and the accountant is mandatory. The bookkeeper is the internal financial manager while the accountant acts as the intermediary between the business and government agencies that oversee business finances.

A CPA can really help map out a plan for summarizing, filing, and analyzing the financial results of the company. Good bookkeeping is evident in profitable, well run organizations.

Accounting has morphed into information organization; it is not just the financial results of business, but access to contracts, customers and referral sources. Transcending access, it includes how information is gathered and used in the company. It starts with management and who does what. Financial transactions, at a minimum, need to be in a bookkeeping software package. Again, a CPA or strong IT (information technology) consultant can plan and implement programs and procedures.

Map out a plan with the accountant so that there are clear guidelines on the back office of the company. Are such items as a point of sale system, job costing, budgeting, or periodic financial statements needed? If running a checkbook, keep copies of everything, and keep them well organized. Often, a bookkeeper or accounting firm can take the checkbook as well as other records and form it into a financial statement.

The key to peace of mind with a bookkeeper is to have them interface with the CPA. Ask the accountant to review the competency of the bookkeeping during the year, so corrections can be implemented before too much time elapses.

Bookkeepers should be expected to:
- Record receipts/payments and complete bank reconciliation (Inquire about segregation of duties)
- File records
- Work out installments for paying vendors
- Complete the Business Activity Statement (BAS)

- Offer training in the use of software
- Collect debts
- Write checks (ready for signature)
- Assist with quotes

Make Fraud Difficult.
A major mistake that many business owners make is allowing the bookkeeper to write checks and do the bank reconciliations. The statistic for small business defalcations resulting in financial loss to the business is one in five. Talk to the CPA specifically about fraud.

Protect Company Data.
Address the issue of backups, both on site and off site. Companies such as Mozy, Carbonite, Barracuda Networks and Rackspace provide off site data back up at a reasonable cost. Be sure to test backups to assure they are working.

48 Choose tax year and accounting method. Corporations may be on fiscal year or calendar year. They may have their books running on a cash basis or an accrual basis. Clearly, working with the accountant is extremely important in determining the answers to these questions.

49 Apply for Federal Tax Identification. For tax purposes, a business needs to have its own Federal Tax Identification Number. A number can be easily accessed by going to www.irs.gov. It may be a good idea to have an accountant or enrolled agent assist in filing out the forms. The IRS has resources to help businesses, including classes and courses for business owners and tax preparers. Business owners can get advice about employee taxes and business taxes.

50 Apply for state employer identification. Some states allow the Federal Tax and State Tax Identification to be the same number. In other states they are separate. Be sure to check with state authorities for the correct procedure.

51 Interview business bankers and select one. I am often asked about the difference between banks. They seem to all provide similar services and loans, so how does one choose over another? I will start by making the point that "they" are not all the same and what is most important is to group banks into major categories: (1) Community banks (sometimes referred to as "regional" banks); (2) Credit Unions; (3) National (large) banks. The differences between them are mostly related to the clients they serve, the level of individual service, loan and bank decision processes, company goals and charters.

Community banks serve local businesses. Local is often determined by the bank's charter and regulator's sign-offs when the bank organizes. While deposits into a large national bank serve people throughout the county and the world, deposits in community banks stay local. Therefore, community bank loan officers tend to be more accessible to their customers and decisions about loans are typically made locally as well. By definition, regulators, legislators and bankers refer to community banks as having less than $1 billion in assets under management. But that is not always the case. The common disadvantage for businesses working with community banks is the number of loan options and funding limitations. However, most companies will never outgrow their local community bank's funding ability.

Credit Unions are non-profit financial cooperatives. By definition, they do not issue stock or pay dividends. What would normally be profit dividends are instead returned to members through lower loan rates, higher interest on deposits and lower fees. Credit unions are exempt from federal and most state taxes because credit unions are member-owned, non-profit organizations generally managed by volunteer board members. People qualify for credit union membership through their employer or affiliations such as churches or social groups.

So the question for a small business owner is does he want to work with a local bank that provides exemplary service, works with local businesses and offers local decision making power? Or would he prefer to get best possible rates by working with a non-profit? Or is he more concerned with working with a large bank with deep pockets that will never outgrow the business? The real business decision is finding the right balance between them all that best fits the situation. (This Step was written, in part, from data retrieved from: www.federalreserve.gov and http://www.cuna.org/gov and http://www.ffiec.gov.)

52 *Open a business bank account.* Be sure to open a business account and not another personal account. It is best if the new business account has overdraft protection and that when creating the account apply for a credit card with the same bank. Unfortunately, customers' checks sometimes bounce. When such instances occur, it is important to build a good relationship with the banker and have protection in place.

When applying for a business checking account, all officers of the company need to be present and the following forms are required:
1. All signers on the account must be present;
2. Business entity filing forms (Articles of Incorporation, for example.);
3. Driver's Licenses of each signer;
4. Federal Tax Identification Number;
5. An initial deposit.

Now that the business account is opened, close the personal account and keep a record of all the transactions which occurred while using the first account.

53 Apply for a business credit card. Now that Step 52 is complete, the banker will likely ask if the business needs a credit card. Absolutely, every business should have one. In this early stage the amount of credit will be determined solely on the basis of the founder's credit score.

54 First draft of business plan completed. By this stage the business should be formalized. The key about this timing is that relatively speaking; the cost of development has been low. Moving forward, the risks grow immensely. Chapter Three of the *Business Owner's Handbook* reviews business planning in great detail. In summary, a business plan identifies all facets of the business. It defines the business, identifies the goals and serves as the firm's resume. Simply put, it is the road map from start-up to business success. Additionally, framing the business in writing makes it real and challenges the entrepreneur to think through all aspects of making the business successful. Having a realistic plan in place puts the mind at ease, gives enthusiasm a boost and sets the subconscious for success. With a written plan in hand, future growth and profits increase exponentially.

55 Define the exit strategy. The exit strategy is further defined in Chapter Three – *Developing A Business Plan*. However, it is a legitimate step in the start-up process to ensure that all the founders agree on what will happen under all circumstances. What happens if the business achieves its goals? What is considered failure? What are the hard-stop points? What are the agreed stages of development? Have buy-sell agreements been discussed? What will occur if a founder becomes sick, ill or injured? If the company achieves it goals should it plan new growth strategies, build horizontally, vertically or consider an initial public offering? All of these issues should be discussed – having the end in mind during the start helps make decision down the road.

56 Review city, county, state and federal agency list. Chapter Six of the *Business Owner's Handbook* outlines many of the possible agencies that can affect the business. Go through the list and demine based on the business model which agencies should be put on the list in order to determine what licenses and permits should be applied for in Step 57.

57 Apply for major licenses and permits. Any person doing business, conducting any trading, calling or practicing any profession within a city is required to apply for a business license. In addition, residential rental properties comprised of four or more units are required to have a business license. (Please note: Business license fees are often based on the number of employees. Therefore, a new business may have to wait until it's determined (and hired) those employees before applying. See Step 109.)

A completed business license application can be submitted to the Information/Cashier counter in the Community Development wing of City Hall. Photo identification for the business owner(s) is required with the application. The public information staff will determine if an inspection is required. (In the event that physical improvements will be made to the building, please contact the Building Department.) The staff will also tabulate fees. Upon receiving final building and planning approval, it will be four to six weeks before the license is received.

Please keep in mind that planning approval is needed *first* and *before* the business license application can be fully processed. Also, depending on the nature of the business, certain types of business licenses require approval from the Police Department.

Administrative Conditional Use Permits - Organizations and other sponsors of temporary, occasional activities or events conducted outdoors are required to obtain an Administrative Conditional Use Permit. Typical activities that require this permit include fund-raising events, outdoor promotional sales, seasonal sales (such as Christmas tree lots) and special public events such as Bingo and Monte Carlo nights.

The purpose of this process is to ensure events are safe and do not significantly affect the welfare of surrounding residents and businesses. Completed applications, along with payment of the fee, must be submitted to the Planning Division at least thirty days prior to the activity. There is no fee for non-profit organizations.

Other agencies may include: Alcohol Beverage Control Board; Environmental Protection Agency; Securities and Exchange Commission; Federal Trade Commission; Department of Commerce; Air Quality Management District; ATF – Alcohol, Tobacco, and Firearms and the Secretary of State

58 Apply for capital (debt or equity). Most businesses need capital to launch successfully. Refer to Chapter Two of the *Business Owner's Handbook* for details.

59 Develop 12-24 month cash flow forecast. When developing the cash flow forecast there should be four "cash-in" line items including revenue, founder's equity cash injection, investor's cash and borrowing base. The four cash-in line items should be staggered over time to show the need to cash when necessary, not all at once in the first month. The cash out should include one-time capital expenditures as well as fixed expenses, variable expenses, payroll, taxes, interest, loan payments and dividends. The cash flow forecast should balance with the use of capital worksheet and the pro forma profit and loss statement.

60 Hire business coach or incubator. As the 125-Steps suggest, there is a lot of work to be done in order to start or acquire a company. Hiring a professional service will usually result in a net savings due to the experience the team brings to the table. Time is money. A professional (like SUMATICI) can typically get through all 125 steps in less than 90 days while it takes most non-professionals up to a year or longer. Unfortunately, most entrepreneurs skip many of the steps in order to save time and money. By doing so, they run the risk of failure down the road.

61 Develop the sales cycle. The sales cycle will define the entire process for working with customers from initial marketing and advertising to the acquisition of the potential buyer. The next step is the first introduction, presenting the sale, closing the sale, delivering the product and/or service, and following-up for customer service, asking for referrals and beginning the cycle again.

62 Develop prototypes. If the business involves products, it is important to build prototypes. Making prototypes is much more expensive than the cost of mass production. There are a number of companies that specialize in making prototypes. A few words of caution:
1. Get references and follow up on them before hiring a prototype company;
2. Ensure a contract exists which includes an agreed price and timeline;
3. Confirm certifications and licenses, when applicable;
4. Ensure a confidentiality statement is signed by the prototype company to protect the business;

5. Ensure the company hired to build the prototype has the proper building materials to make the prototype accurately. Prototype companies are a small niche community and many times are willing to refer each other if they cannot provide the service.

63 Develop a specific customer list. Developing a specific target market list is like shooting a rifle instead of a shotgun – one shot, one target. Many companies make the mistake of spending tens of thousands of dollars - or more! - on mass marketing when very often a targeted list is much more efficient. Because entrepreneurs see how *Future 500* companies implement their marketing campaigns, they assume this is the right thing to do. But it is not. Buying lists form professional companies is a good use of marketing capital. When being interviewed by a vendor be sure that the seller knows the company's target market's demographics, geographical data and provides a current list.

64 Start test markets. Once prototypes have been manufactured, conduct test marketing. Let potential customers try the product/service(s) - for free, if possible. Gather as much feedback as possible. Place all the test materials and results into a booklet which will be added to the business plan under "Supporting Documents."

65 Track test market data. After making adjustments from the first test, offer the product/service(s) again. Gather feedback to see if there is measurable improvement. Keep the test materials and results with the first test marketing documents.

66 Interview intellectual property lawyers. During the interview be sure to ask for track record results, cost for paying the attorney and filing fees. A typical agreement includes a retainer, initial search results, filing and follow-up.

Ongoing protection may be part of the agreement as well. Some will charge a flat rate and others by the hour. Most professionals charge by the hour. It is important that an intellectual property (IP) attorney is hired, not an attorney that may complete IP projects part time. This will be a long-time relationship so ensure the attorney hired is likeable.

67 File for intellectual property protection. Trademark rights are established by either using the mark or filing a proper application to register a mark with the U.S. Patent and Trademark Office (PTO). While registering with the PTO is not necessary for establishing trademark rights, registering the mark can help secure benefits, such as an official notice of a claim to the mark, evidence of ownership, the ability to invoke federal court jurisdiction, a basis for obtaining registration in foreign countries and preventing the importation of infringing foreign goods. The registration process generally takes six months from start to finish.

Copyrighting creative work protects it from unauthorized use. With a registered copyright, the owner controls how the work is reproduced, distributed and presented publicly. Copyright is a form of protection grounded in the U.S. Constitution and granted by law for original works of authorship fixed in a tangible medium of expression. Copyright covers both published and unpublished works.

A patent cannot be obtained on a mere idea or suggestion. Patent applications are examined for both technical and legal merit. A utility patent may be granted to anyone who invents or discovers any new and useful process, machine, article of manufacture, compositions of matter, or any new useful improvement thereof. A design patent may be granted to anyone who invents a new, original and ornamental design for an article of manufacture.

68 Start management and operations plan. Questions to consider when developing the operational and management plan should include integration of the sales cycle of business by determining the length of time it takes to build, create ship and sell. A fact of life is that 'operations' is never happy with sales: too much in sales and they cannot produce, too little in sales and the company is going out of business. The step includes the development of an organizational chart with the management team.

69 Create a PowerPoint about the Company. Develop a sales presentation for the product/service(s). It should be developed for vendors, customers, employees and capital providers. Practice on family, friends and business associates. Create a list of objections. Note the weaknesses and rough spots and prepare more presentations until it is perfected.

70 Interview manufactures and vendors. When considering where to purchase supplies and stock, it is important to investigate all the manufacturers and distributors in the industry through letters, email, catalogs and trade shows. This provides a fair assessment of pricing, shipping, availability and professionalism. If seeking their business advice, it's a good idea to bring them in on the company ideas early in the business planning process. The good ones will help steer the company to success and help to avoid pitfalls of the industry.

71 Define ethics and community program. In today's business environment it is standard operating procedure to create an ethics and community program. This includes such concepts as "Being Green," serving the community through service clubs and keeping a balance of business needs and community needs. Putting these concepts into practice early in the business development cycle is key to long term success.

72 *Interview real estate agents and hire one.* A commercial real estate agent is the most qualified person for this step. Lengthy contracts, agreements and inspections must be accomplished as part of this step.

73 *Research cities for operations.* Be sure to check with the City Community Development Department. When choosing a city be sure to consider:
1. Costs and limitations relating to the opening of a new business or move an existing new location;
2. City requirements relating to increasing the seating or floor space area, hours of operation or alterations of existing business in any way;
3. Limitation related to exterior or interior alterations, or other modifications to an existing building (including partition walls over five feet in height, plumbing, heating system, electrical system, and mechanical system, etc.);
4. Issues to displaying of any new signs or modifying an existing sign(s);
5. Ease in the process for storing, producing or using combustibles, toxic substances, corrosives, explosives or pressurized gases in the conduct of business;
6. Business friendliness of the city;
7. Streamline processes for applications;
8. Business Assistance programs.

74 *Investigate zoning and entitlements.* Where will the business be located? Is it retail, service or manufacturing? Is it going to be in a commercial location or home-based? Is the possible location zoned correctly for that type of business? To ensure access to all the information needed to establish a new business in the chosen city, there are some important things to know. Before doing *anything*, please talk to City staff. The first necessary step to ensure that all City requirements are addressed is to check whether the business use is permitted at a given location within the City. The land zoning district regulates permissible uses. In some cases, the use may not be permitted at all. Problems arise when property is leased or construction initiated without first checking with City staff. Be honest and clear about proposal so that the City staff can help achieve the company's objectives. They will do their best to ensure access to all the necessary information to legally establish the business, including different options that may be available in obtaining approvals.

Building permits are required in order to build, modify, remove or repair all structures in a city. This includes everything from new buildings to block walls, roofs and signs. Once a complete set of project plans has been approved by the Development Services Team, a building permit will be issued for the project. Building permit fees vary according to the type of construction and number of stories, or the length of time needed to perform the inspection of the proposed construction.

It is important to determine if the business has any of the following environmentally sensitive issues that require further investigation and applications for permits: (1) Air quality; (2) Hazardous waste; (3) Ground water contamination; (4) Underground storage.

75 Review all location options. Now that multiple cities have been interviewed, properties assessed, entitlement reviewed, and pros and cons surmised, it is time to choose the location. Make a list and include lifestyle issues. It is often smart to work and live in the same community. This is a major milestone.

76 Contact utility companies. When contacting the utilities, be prepared to answer the same type of questions as when filling out the application for a business bank account: responsible parties, corporate tax identification, business entity and the type of business. Ensure when registering with a new utility to ask questions about energy benefits or business programs for the company. There are many programs available that are not offered unless asked for.

77 Choose business headquarters - execute. Business location is very important. Make the decision after a lot of planning and thought. Most importantly, use a professional to help. Contact a commercial realtor for assistance.

78 Interview website developers and choose one. When considering a website developer there are a number of decisions to make. Does the company specialize in design or programming? Do they include domain purchasing, hosting, maintenance and upgrades? Do they build a site from a platform or from a template? Do they build social media, Meta tagging, social media and search engine optimization into the site when building it? Do they charge a flat rate or by the hour?

79 Interview insurance companies. Business insurance - Having the right insurance coverage is a must for any business owner. Liability insurance is needed to protect the business. Business insurance will protect business property in the event of a catastrophe. Also purchase insurance for employees to cover any mistakes that may cause damage to a client or to themselves. Look into having professional insurance called "errors and omissions insurance."

Workers Compensation Insurance – In most states, every company is required to have Worker's Compensation Insurance. The cost is based on a percentage of the wages paid. Worker's Compensation helps protect the company and the employee in the event an employee is hurt, disabled or otherwise unable to perform his/her duties due to injury.

Life Insurance, Key Man Insurance and Buy-Sell Agreements - In the event of a business owner's or key manager's death, "Key Man" insurance will provide the financing to pay off the business interests of the officer and his or her family so the business may continue after the untimely death.

Health insurance - Contact a number of companies to receive bids on health insurance. The plans and options are confusing and a professional should be consulted to make the choices for company officers as well as the employees.

80 Purchase all applicable insurance policies. Once all the interviews have taken place in Step 79, choose a firm to work with. The best case scenario is to have one company handle all the policies. It is usually less expensive to bundle the plans and one point of contact is easier to manage.

81 Register with State and Federal agencies. Once applications are submitted it is a good idea to stay in contact with them, and once ready for operations, notify them of the intent to begin operations activate applications. Review Chapter Six for the list of agencies.

82 Turn on all utilities: electric, water and gas. When registering ensure the bills are created under the name of the business and the federal tax identification number. Be prepared for deposits as businesses typically pay large deposits as compared to personal accounts.

83 Turn on phone, media and internet. Consider all the available resources for company communications, internally

and externally. Here is a sample of decisions that will need to be made concerning communications:
1. Basic Local Business Phone Service;
2. Local Basic Phone Service;
3. Long Distance Carrier;
4. Mobile Service;
5. Broadband Internet Service Provider;
6. Website;
7. Long Distance;
8. Toll Free Numbers.

Toll Free Number Options. If the business intends to have a toll-free number, try to make the number compatible to the business. This will help with branding (Such as 800-busines). Try www.tollfreenumbers.com.

Voice Over IP. VOIP uses existing high-speed internet connection to allow the user to make and receive phone calls to any phone in the world. Try www.skype.com.

Webinar. This service enables the user to manage meetings or conduct trainings through the phone and Internet. Try www.gotomeeting.com.

Conference Calling. This enables the user to have a conference call instantly, anywhere, with up to 125 participants for only 4 cents a minute, per user. Try www.starconferencing.com.

Mobile Phones. Contact a carrier and let them know about the need to set up a business account. DO NOT get a "family plan" for business use. Do not mix personal cell phone usage with business cell phone usage. Further, it is not a good idea to have employees use their personal phones for business use.

Email. Have email addresses match the website.

84 Complete the marketing plan. Having defined the product or service; the market; the promotion approach and the Marketing Communications Plan (MarComm plan), now determine how to sell. Develop final document planning for:
1. Direct sales (commission or salary);
2. Representative sales;
3. Web, mail order or phone sales;
4. TV infomercial;
5. To wholesalers;
6. To retailers.

The cost of the sales approach is an important element of enterprise cost structure and product price. The lack of sales will put the company out of business. What is the universe of customers and how the sales funnel is managed is key to management.

How does public perception fit into the product or service? Public Relations could play a big role in selling. The rule of thumb for a marketing budget is 10% of the cash flow and sales forecasting. The 10% rule should always apply. It should be broken down into three categories:

- Branding. When a business is first getting started, three to four percent of the budget should be in branding. Branding means recognition. It means money spent so that the buyers know the company name and the type of business it is.
- Advertising. Two to three percent should be budgeted for advertising. Advertising is the "call to action" you want the customer to perform. It provides the product and the company name, but most importantly it tells the customer to "come and get it."
- Customer Retention Management (CRM). Three to four percent of the budget should be spent on Customer Retention Management, a key aspect of

marketing which many companies fail to focus on. Once brand loyalty is built through branding, keeping the customer over the lifespan of the business is the challenge. To put it plainly, branding means recognition, advertising is a call to action and CRM keeps customers coming back.

Here is a list of typical marketing products to consider for a business marketing plan:
1. Promotional Products;
2. Promotional Gifts;
3. Corporate Gifts;
4. Greeting Cards;
5. Database Management;
6. Reminder Systems;
7. Gift Cards;
8. Sponsorship Opportunities;
9. Birthday Gifts;
10. Holiday Gifts;
11. Anniversary Gifts and
12. Referral Gifts.

As the business grows successfully, less money should be in branding and more in customer retention management.

After many years of business, the ratio will become two percent for branding, four percent for advertising and four percent in customer retention management.

85 Make contact with potential vendors. At this phase of development it is time to choose the vendors, sign contracts and begin building services and/or inventories.

86 Design a company logo. The logo is one of the first steps in branding a business. It should be designed for a number of formats including, but not limited to print media, web media and high and low resolution. It should have at least two colors. If possible, the name should be represented. A graphic artist can help design the logo.

87 Design branding concepts. The lender and/or investor expect the business plan to inform him how the company will 'promote' products or services. The promotion strategy is driven by: (1) The specific product or service; (2) The market segment the company is engaged in; (3) The competitive forces at play.

A Marketing Communications Plan (MarComm) is a living document that should cover:
1. Print advertising;
2. Trade shows;
3. Collateral (brochures etc.);
4. Promotional items;
5. Press releases;
6. Editorial article program;
7. Memberships.

Branding the business is vital. Create a plan that will give the business a special identity which will create a positive energy about the business with buyers. Public perception is critical. Branding and advertising must work together. Advertisements should include the logo, tag lines and a consistent message to buyers. The website, business name, logo and even the phone number (if possible) should all reflect the same message.

88 Review public relations considerations. Will the company need internet based public relations or traditional programs for building and protecting the company's reputation. Is the PR plan in coordination with the marketing plan for press leases?

89 *Develop the advertising plan.* Three to four percent of the budget should be spent on advertising. Advertising is a call to action: the buyer is asked to respond (redeem a coupon; participate in a sale, etc.).

90 *Approve the company logo and branding.* Besides logos, a graphic designer will develop stationery, letterhead, envelopes, business cards, flyers, brochures, website designs and other marketing materials. A graphic artist will be one of the most important consultants hired. When choosing a graphic artist, review his/her portfolio and check references and referrals.

91 *Join the Chamber of Commerce.* Joining the Chamber is one of the most important investments a business owner can make. The return on investment is incalculable. Being in the Chamber will provide many benefits including:
1. Providing research and business statistics;
2. Connections to government agencies;
3. Connections to planning departments;
4. Direction to the correct city departments and personnel;
5. Introductions to other business leaders in the community.

Other benefits include: Network opportunities through monthly breakfast or luncheon meetings, or through monthly mixers; Legislative Action Committees that keep members informed of pertinent legislative actions that may affect business; Referral and reference systems in place for when the public calls; Business training; Representation in the local city government (without city funding for the chamber); Grand Opening Ribbon Cutting ceremonies; Introduction to civic leadership at both cities, local and state levels; Monthly newsletters.

92 *Make contact with potential customers*. Start the sales cycle with potential customers – use Steps 61, 63, 64, 86, 89 and 91 to complete the contact with customers.

93 *Interview architects and designers*. If the business needs tenant improvements or construction it is important to get bids from at least three companies before choosing one. Ensure to get references for all of them – and call the references to ask about timeliness, ability to stay on budget and professionalism.

94 *Hire a team for building or improvements*. Once Step 95 is complete hire the company chosen, pay the retainer costs and get started.

95 *Apply for building permits*. The contractor should assist in this regard. One of the biggest hold-ups in business start-up and development is the permitting process. Plan for the worst and hope for the best. Hold everyone accountable.

96 *Apply for resale permit*. If the company is selling anything that requires the collection of sales tax, it will need a resale permit. One of the biggest mistakes made by business owners is not handling sales tax professionally and properly. Through the resale permit, the state allows a business to collect taxes on the items that business sells. Collected sales taxes must be reported on a quarterly basis to the State Board of Equalization. The State Board of Equalization usually conducts seminars including Basic Sales Tax and Tax Preparation Return. Check your State Board of Equalization's website for a seminar schedule.

97 *Apply for a surety bond*. In accordance with the rules of the State Board of Equalization, a business must also apply for a bond which protects the state in the event the business defaults on sales tax payments.

98 Build the facility or finish improvements. Consult with a general contractor, handyman and an interior designer. Planning is key. Have the contractors review the marketing plan and the branding plan so the business place has a feel that matches the entire branding plan of the company.

99 Install fixtures, furniture and equipment. Now that the city has been chosen, the utilities turned on, and the business is ready to launch, order and install the fixtures furniture and equipment.

100 Order and install signage. Use a well respected firm that is recommended by the local chamber of commerce. Since this is a one-time install of a sign that may be up for decades, the decision is important.

101 Call vendors to order initial inventory. Since vendors have already been interviewed and the scope of work defined in earlier stages this should only be a matter of creating a purchase order and accepting the shipment.

102 Stock the office with necessary supplies. Office supplies are a constant consumable and should be put on an ongoing refill ordering system so that the company has all the necessary supplies form the first day. The initial order will likely include one-time expense such as small electric utility equipment, garbage cans, coffee makers and other one-time expenses. Buy in bulk as the company will need it and the cost each is significant such as paper, note pads, etc.

103 Start the staff interview process. Write out a description in advance of the type of personnel the company is looking for. Choosing a staff with good synergy is important. Build a team from the beginning. When interviewing, a good idea is to give a brief description of the company, its goals and the expectations of the position the person is interviewing for.

Give interviewers plenty of time to give notices to their current employers. Two weeks is standard. When interviewing, plan a month ahead to get through the process. Hiring a background check company is important as well.

104 Interview payroll companies. Payroll companies can provide many advantages to a small business owner including filing employment taxes, managing paychecks, processing ongoing payroll forms, issuing checks, run background checks on employees and many other services. Some will also implement employee benefit programs and assist in the hiring process. Some are not only payroll companies but offer services such as Professional Employee Organizations (PEOs) in which they hire the employees and lease them back to the company. This is designed to reduce liability and lower workers compensation costs.

105 Implement the marketing plan. At this point in the process the planning is over. The business plan should be complete and the implementation process should begin. This person or company will assist in the launching of the business. A business plan implementation specialist will assist the company to stay on target with goals and the budget, and will act as a liaison with vendors, contractors, employees and the government agencies. Essentially, this is a project manager hired to launch the company.

106 Website live to the public. Now that the company is about to launch, the website should be live to the public. Ensure the marketing, public relations and contact information on the site is all live and ready for immediate reaction if contacts are made through the web.

107 Interview and hire a printing company. Having a strong and trusted relationship with a printer is strategically important to every business. When working with a printer, look for the following: (1) Does the printer understand the marketing plan? (2) Provide a budget in advance and ensure the printer can stay within the budget; (3) Find out if the printer over/undercharges; (4) Ensure the printer is conscious of the deadlines and can commit to them; (5) Ask many questions about price in terms of color, quantity discounts, type of paper, etc.

108 Implement social media plan. Now that the website is live and the marketing plan is in full implementation the social media plan should be implemented as well. Both the company officers and the company itself should have social media accounts that are all linked for increased traffic. For further information refer to the marketing section of the Handbook.

109 Apply for a city business license. The business license may be applied for earlier than this Step. (See Step 57.) However, since the business is now ready to launch, the employees are hired and the business will begin selling, now is the time to apply. The reason is that most licenses are based on the number of employees or projected sales or both.

110 Select a credit card merchant service. This is one of the most confusing and complicated decisions to make regarding business finances. Once the fictitious name is submitted a flurry of companies will offer "merchant services" with an array of overwhelming options. When hiring a merchant services company ask the following questions:

1. Do I buy the machine, rent it or lease it?
2. How long is the contract?
3. What happens if I close my business before the contract expires?

4. Can I skip the machine and process credit cards on line?
5. Does the company process customer's credit cards using a banks processor or its own?
6. What fees will I pay and how are they assessed?
7. Are there minimum/maximum charges?
8. Do the clients have to be present to charge their cards?
9. What is the difference between the processor, the merchant services provider, the approval company and the bank?
10. Can I just get a web-based account?
11. Do you provide mobile services?
12. How long does it take to get paid once batches are sent?

111 Design policies and procedures. There are companies that provide these kinds of services. It is vitally important to establish policies, rules and regulations in advance. Most employee disputes are resolved far in advance if the expectations are established from the beginning. In addition, Federal and State Employment posters should be purchased and posted before any staff begins working for the company. The posters and all public employee information are to be posted in a conspicuous place.

112 Start hiring. Report employee information to the Employment Development Department (EDD). Under state law, employers are required to report specific information periodically. Some states require that even if the company pays no wages during a quarter, it is still considered an employer and required to sign and file the *Quarterly Wage and Withholding Report* (DE 6). Please refer to the EDD website for more information on your state's requirements.

In order for any business to run effectively and efficiently it needs the right personnel serving in the right positions. In small businesses this is especially true because individual employees have a greater impact. The small business owner needs to identify and recruit qualified employees with the right skills and capabilities to match the company's ongoing and future needs. In the employer/employee relationship, the business owner also needs to comply with local, state and federal regulations governing that relationship. All these things come under the category of "Human Resources" (HR). HR includes:

- Maintaining awareness of and compliance with local, state and federal labor laws
- Recruitment, selection, and on boarding (resourcing)
- Employee record-keeping and confidentiality
- Organizational design and development
- Business transformation and change management
- Performance, conduct and behavior management
- Industrial and employee relations
- Human resources (workforce) analysis and workforce personnel data management
- Compensation and employee benefit management
- Training and development (learning management)
- Employee motivation and morale-building (employee retention and loyalty)

The first step in getting a company's human resources in order is being clear on the company's structure. The following are simple organizational charts which can be used as templates to get a business owner started. In order to design an organizational chart, think about what your business is trying to do and answer how the company will accomplish that goal(s) through its employees.

Once the company organization has been identified, begin identifying the skills each employee needs to function at each level through writing job descriptions including the tasks and responsibilities carried out by each employee.

The next step is deciding how much each employee is to be paid. Fortunately, most states' Employment Development Department (EDD) provide a breakdown of employee positions, with a general description of each and a salary range for the inexperienced, new hire, to medium, to experienced. For example, on the California EDD website (www.caljobs.ca.gov) has an "Occupational Guides" section that allows searches by keyword. Once an occupation is identified, the vital information about that occupation is provided. By developing the organizational chart and being specific about the skills and capabilities of each employee, the business owner can decide what experience level he needs each position needs, and then can budget for his future payroll.

When recruiting employees, businesses are affected by both internal and external factors. External factors are generally out of the business owner's control and include such things as the economic climate and current and future labor market trends. We've already discussed some of the major internal factors, but others include the organizational culture, underpinned by management style, environmental climate and the approach to ethical and corporate social responsibilities.

To know the business environment a business operates in, three major trends must be considered:

1. Demographics: the characteristics of a population/workforce, for example, age, gender or social class. This type of trend may have an effect in relation to pension offerings, insurance packages etc.
2. Diversity: the variation within the population/workplace. Changes in society now mean

that a larger proportion of organizations are made up of "baby-boomers" or older employees in comparison to thirty years ago. Advocates of "workplace diversity" simply advocate an employee base that is a mirror reflection of the make-up of society insofar as race, gender, sexual orientation etc.

3. Skills and qualifications: as industries move from manual to more managerial professions so does the need for more highly skilled graduates. If the market is "tight" (i.e. not enough staff for the jobs), employers must compete for employees by offering financial rewards, community investment, etc.

Another factor to consider is the make-up of the employee market and the individuals who make up that market. For example:

- Geographical spread: how far is the job from the individual? The distance to travel to work should be in line with the pay offered, and the transportation and infrastructure of the area also influence who applies for a post.

- Occupational structure: the norms and values of the different careers within an organization. There are three different types of occupational structure, namely, craft (loyalty to the profession), organization career (promotion through the firm) and unstructured (lower/unskilled workers who work when needed).

- Generational difference: different age categories of employees have certain characteristics which will affect their behavior and their expectations of the organization. For example, a "baby boomer" (someone born between 1946-1964) employee has a strong work ethic that leans more towards "putting in the hours" whereas a "Generation X" (1965-1980) employee's work ethic is more like "work to live, don't live to work." Those different generational attitudes will affect their attitude towards their employment and their employer.

Many small businesses don't have the capital resources to maintain an in-house HR department to handle all the employee record keeping required by the different levels of government. Fortunately, there are companies and services available which can, for a reasonable fee, take care of these responsibilities. We recommend the entrepreneur research what's available and incorporate plans for HR needs into his business plan. SUMATICI can help.

113 Start training new staff members. Be sure to research workforce resources – education, training and placement. The search should begin with the utilization of free resources. Identify the training level required such as unskilled or skilled and also identify the potential employee's education level needed for the position(s) to be filled. The EDD can help a business find skilled workers, stay competitive and make informed decisions. The EDD offers a full array of job placement services, up-to-date information on the labor market and emerging occupations, tax and hiring incentives and more. Their website is www.edd.ca.gov/employer.htm.

114 Host a pre-grand opening event. It is a good idea to have a pre-grand opening. Invite family, friends, employees and employee families. This provides for a good "dry-run" before inviting the public so the managers can work out the "bugs" and ensure the business is "ready to roll."

115 Assess lessons learned. The purpose of the pre-grand opening is to ensure the company is operating at its optimum. Hold a team meeting and review the lessons learned.

116 Start selling – buy contact manager. There are many contact management systems. One of the best on the market is *Sales Force* (see www.salesforce.com). The sales cycle should be in full force at this stage.

117 Start customer retention management (CRM). The contact management software should also include customer retention management systems. A system for thanking customers, customer referrals and ensuring all company contact systems are linked are all part of a solid CRM system.

118 Contact local economic partnership. The Economic Development Council may be a company's connection to the leadership and resources of the city. A non-profit corporation representing public and private sectors, the Partnership is a good source for new and existing business owners to gain city-specific information, expertise, consulting, services and events.

119 Implement operations and marketing. The company should be in full swing and operations at this stage with the marketing team selling and the operations team fulfilling orders.

120 Make public announcements. Another marketing factor to consider is Public Relations. Public Relations deal with the public's knowledge of a company's humanitarian and/or philanthropic efforts, and could play a big role in selling. How does public perception (shaped by the Public Relations efforts) fit in with the company's product or service? Again, all marketing and branding should tie together and deliver a unified message.

121 Begin regulatory compliance procedures. Any permits and licensing that require ongoing reporting should be implemented now that the sales and operations team is in full operation. This may be as simple as reporting the fact the operation have begun but for some businesses regulatory compliance includes daily or weekly inspections and reporting.

122 Join peer and networking groups. There are hundreds of networking meetings held throughout the country on a weekly basis. Joining these networking organizations is an excellent way to promote a small business. They include, but are not limited to: (1) Business Network International (BNI); (2) The TEAM Referral Network (teamreferralnetwork.com); (3) Worthwhile Referral Service (WSI); (4) Networking breakfasts, luncheons, and mixers; (5) Meeting and Mixers (www.meetingsandmixers.com); (7) Vistage; (8) Industry associations.

123 Hold a grand opening event. The Chamber of Commerce will help plan a great event including a ribbon cutting ceremony. Also consider hiring an events planner so the managers can focus on meeting people and not worry about the details.

124 Submit press releases. Announce the opening of the business, key strategic alliances, customers and special announcements.

125 Reset goals, evaluate and adjust. Follow the business plan, re-write and update it as conditions change, stay disciplined and stay focused on the long term strategies and short term tactics.

~ A Hero ~

Here we share the story of Phil Pace – co-founder and operator of *Phil's BBQ* in the San Diego area of Southern California. Not only does Phil exude the qualities of a successful entrepreneur, he is the prime example of what we mean when we describe a "Hero."

Phil grew up in a family of restaurateurs and started his first restaurant when he was 18, in Painesville, Ohio. He got the idea for creating his own BBQ sauce from his enjoyment of eating pork ribs cooked in his family's spaghetti sauce recipe. After moving to California in 1992, he found a small restaurant space available in Mission Hills (San Diego) and decided to open a small BBQ business with his friend, Jeff Loya. *Phil's BBQ* operates in the hospitality industry, fast-casual, restaurant sector, earning revenue serving mesquite wood grilled BBQ. The company has been successful because it mass produces quality food by focusing on a limited menu with limited line items producing an award winning cuisine with quality and consistency as its main draw for an industry record of repeat customers and market penetration.

Their success required moving into a larger facility – sales grew every year for 12 years in a row. The restaurant originally opened in an 800 square foot facility in 1998. Phil and his team have won numerous awards for both restaurant services and community philanthropic works, including: Restaurateur of the Year by the California Restaurant Association, Caterer of the Year by the San Diego Union Tribune Reader's Poll, Winner "Cities Best BBQ – San Diego AOL City Guide Poll," Winner "Best Restaurant," "Winner - Best BBQ" and dozens of other awards.

And if all that is not enough, you need to know the story behind the story. Was it easy to make his business a success?

No way. He and Jeff have dealt with every conceivable roadblock and knock them down, one-by-one, day-by-day. Challenges? You bet. From air quality control board issues that were solved by designing a custom smoke filtration system to the every-day property, payroll, taxes, workers compensation and staffing issues plagued by all entrepreneurs. Phil deals with issues that most would not or cannot. Can you imagine the level of organization it takes serving thousands of meals in a day in one location, ordering the right product, ensuring your team and equipment are running to optimum levels all day and night – for more than a decade straight?

Today, Phil employs more than 200 people in the San Diego area, serves thousands of meals per day, and runs his operation with speed, agility, flexibility and fairness with unequalled enthusiasm and commitment. He pays his taxes, pays his bills and indirectly and directly affects tens of thousands of people in San Diego. Why was Phil's story first on our list of heroes? It's not only because he runs the best BBQ house in America. It's not only because he donates to charity organizations. It's because he demands a commitment to success of himself and the people around him.

I recently ran into Phil at a catering event 100 miles from his headquarters late on a Saturday night. Phil was supervising the event like it was any other. I asked him, "What are you doing here? You should be sipping a Corona on a beach somewhere basking in your success." His response, "This is what I do. My success comes from caring about customers, taking a stake in our quality, and caring enough to stay engaged and never taking our success for granted." We agree with him – he is a true American hero – we salute him.

CHAPTER 2
ACCESS TO BUSINESS CAPITAL

Introduction. Accessing business capital options includes six fundamental sources: (1) Owner equity; (2) Personal credit; (3) Company debt by borrowing (loans); (4) Equity – selling part of the company for cash; (5) Grants – sharing information for cash; (6) Royalty – advances on future sales. Most often, raising capital includes a combination of sources. Each form of capital has advantages and disadvantages that are often similar in their basic form with some level of differentiation, but each source is uniquely different as well. The two main sources of the six options are in the form of debt and equity.

While there are stringent federal guidelines about how banks and other lenders conduct business, there are no definitive standards as to how the various types of business loans are structured: terms and conditions may vary from one lender to the next, and minimum and maximum amounts can differ. A borrower is advised to know exactly what conditions apply to each loan being considering.

Owner Equity. Almost any access to capital provider will require owner equity. Put simply, owner equity is personally sourced cash invested in the business. It can also be sourced as collateral against personally owned assets such as:
1. Cash saving;
2. Retirement accounts;
3. Whole life insurance policies;
4. Home equity;
5. Certificates of deposit;
6. Money market accounts;
7. Checking accounts;
8. and personal lines of credit.

Coming from the capital sources perspective, owner equity is all about mitigation of risk and ensuring that the founders and owners have a fair balance of risk as compared to the capital provider. The phrase most often referred to in describing owner equity is having, "skin in the game."

As a consulting firm, we find owner equity to be one of the biggest challenges in working with entrepreneurs because sometimes they do not have enough equity to justify the amount of money being sought. There are objective equity requirements established for most debt sources. For equity capital there tends be more of a subjective, case by case requirement of owner equity.

All capital providers will require transparency regarding the owner's financial situation, clear understanding of the need for capital and that the type of capital is suitable. One of the biggest mistakes we often see is that an owner has exhausted all of his resources, then starts seeking capital. Due to pride or lack of knowledge, the owner thinks that by going broke he is sharing his enthusiasm, risk, belief in the business and commitment; in other words, it's a badge of honor. However, capital providers see it as irresponsible, a lack of planning and a lack of balance between optimism and realism. The point is: seek capital before it is needed to show a high level of business acumen and responsibility. Desperation does not look good on anyone! Here are some examples of personal debt options:

Character Loan. A character loan is a type of unsecured loan that is made on the basis of the borrower's reputation and credit. Borrowers are typically able to obtain only small loans by this method, since, if the borrower is unable to repay the loan, the bank will most likely encounter considerable difficulty in recovering the loaned funds.

Home Equity Lines of Credit. HELOCs were very popular in North America during the real estate boom of 2002-06. However, as housing prices collapsed and homeowners' equity shrank drastically, some lenders increasingly resorted to reductions and revocations of such credit facilities.

Personal Line of Credit and Credit Cards. Credit card advances - in lending, this phrase does not mean taking out cash through a business credit card, although many businesses do that. Instead, it's a loan based on a company's track record and its expected future business. It's a good choice if a business has at least a three-year history of accepting credit cards. Because credit card sales are such a good estimation of future earnings a company will be able to get a fairly good rate on a loan against its expected income.

Personal Loans. This is often the case when raising seed (early) stage capital for a company. Family and friends loan money to the founders. Typically, the loan terms are flexible, based on a repayment of the loan after the company is in full operation. Unfortunately, this form of financing is used often, but rarely organized well. It is important that all loans, regardless of the source be well documented and the terms clearly identified. This is true for a couple of reasons: (1) it maintains the family relationship; and (2) future capital providers will need to review all previous financing including personal loans provided by family and friends.

As the saying goes, "debt is cheaper than equity." The thought behind that popular statement is that if the business is going to achieve the success expected by the founders, then the cost of paying back investors is greater than the cost of interest paid on debt. For that reason, we will start by discussing debt as the primary source of capital.

The 5 C's of Credit. Generally speaking, when applying for a loan, lenders look for the five "C's":

1. Capital – this is owner equity;
2. Character/Credit – Experience, training, willingness to make the business success – history in willingness to pay debt, commonly defined by a fico score;
3. Collateral – Have a secondary source of repayment to cover potential loss;
4. Capacity/Cash Flow – Does the revenue exceed the expenses, and if not, how long will it take;
5. Conditions – How is the market? How is the industry, sector and sub sector doing?

Capital. Capital is the money an owner personally has invested in the business and is an indication of how much the owner will lose should the business fail. Prospective lenders and investors will expect the owner to contribute his own assets and to undertake personal financial risk to establish the business before asking them to commit any funding. If an owner has a significant personal investment in the business he is more likely to do everything in his power to make the business successful. The latest qualifying standard from *Wells Fargo, Citibank, Bank of America, Certified Federal* and others is a request of up to 50% of the capital needed for the business comes from the owners, based on the business model, industry, collateral and an assessment of the other considerations. A rule of thumb is that as owner equity goes down, risk to the lender goes up, thereby requiring a higher qualification standard for borrowing.

Character/Credit. "Character" is the technical term used by lenders about credit and history on the borrower such as employment, training and education. These are both objective and subjective decisions made by lenders and are constantly changing based on the market and the type of borrowing. The lender decides objectively subjectively whether or not the borrower is sufficiently trustworthy to repay the loan or generate a return on funds invested in the company. The quality of past successes, references, background and experience of the borrower, partners with more than 10% ownership, management and key employees may all be considered.

Although the Small Business Administration's (SBA) most important factor is the ability to repay, the character question tends to be the most important factor in today's market. The combination of a strong business plan, five years of experience in the industry and a 680 or high credit score are the keys to providing clear character.

Collateral. We are finding that collateral values have dropped significantly. Only 25-70% of the current value of the collateral may be used. For instance, a home worth $500,000 with a current mortgage of $300,000, leaving $200,000 in equity may only have a collateralized value of $150,000 in the eyes of the lender because of dropping home values. In addition, equity and inventory assets have even lesser collateral value. Trucks, heavy equipment, fixtures and furniture assets will only have 50% of their value applied to the collateral value. Stock and bonds only rate 50% of their value for collateral. Note that these numbers vary by the bank chosen, market conditions and other variables – but the point is that to the uninformed, the assumption that 100% of available equity in collateral is not a reasonable expectation when working with lenders. Perishable inventory has no value. Standard vehicles have little value. Generally, only certificates of deposit receive 100% of their fixed value for collateral.

Collateral or guarantees are additional forms of security a borrower can provide the lender. If the business cannot repay its loan, the bank wants to know there is a second source of repayment. Assets such as equipment, buildings, accounts receivable and in some cases, inventory, are considered possible sources of repayment if they are sold by the bank for cash. Both business and personal assets can be sources of collateral for a loan. A guarantee, on the other hand, is just that - someone else signs a guarantee document promising to repay the loan if the borrower can't. Some lenders may require such a guarantee in addition to collateral as security for a loan.

Capacity. While lenders seek a balance of the five "Cs" of credit, capacity to repay is most often the most critical. The prospective lender will want to know exactly how the borrower intends to repay the loan. The lender will consider the cash flow from the business, the timing of the repayment and the probability of successful repayment of the loan. Payment history on existing credit relationships - personal and commercial - is considered an indicator of future payment performance. Prospective lenders also will want to know contingent sources of repayment in the event of business failure. The business plan should address this through a well formulated assumption worksheets and pro forma profit and loss statements.

Conditions. Conditions include macro economics (global/national), micro (state/local) economics and the business itself. Conditions focus on the intended purpose of the loan. Will the money be used for working capital, additional equipment or inventory? The lender will also consider the economic climate and conditions both within the industry and in other industries that could affect the business. The strength of the business plan and use of funds is important in this regard. How the money is used and the strength of the return on investment argument is high.

Debt Options. Depending on market conditions, traditional business loans are revered for existing businesses with at least three years of records to show proof of the ability to pay. As the economy improves, the minimum number of years may drop to two years. Business loans available for those looking to start a new business are limited. That is why the Federal government offers some small business loans through the Small Business Administration (SBA). This is done in an effort to stimulate the economy thereby creating new jobs and expanding the tax base.

Types of Debt
(Alphabetical)

Accounts Receivable Financing (Factoring & Receivables). Another option for many small businesses is factoring, also known as receivables financing. Factoring is basically selling company invoices to a third party, a finance or factoring company which assumes the risk and provides cash to a business during a time of short cash flow. Instead of waiting for customers to pay, the company can get the funds immediately - minus a small fee (three to five percent) due to the factoring company. Typically a business will receive 80% of the invoice value upfront and the remaining value once the client pays. The amount of money paid to the business varies based upon the age of the invoices or receivables. A more current item will pay more, while a less current item will pay less. Any accounts receivable that are older than 90 days are usually not financed.

A business might be a good candidate for factoring if it has: (1) Fewer than three years in business; (2) Good growth prospects but less than stellar cash flow; (3) Active accounts but slow paying customers.

Acquisition Loan. A loan given to a company to purchase a specific asset or to be used for purposes that are laid out before the loan is granted. The acquisition loan is typically only used for a short window of time, and only for specific purposes. Once repaid, funds available through an acquisition loan cannot be re-borrowed as with a revolving line of credit at a bank. Acquisition loans are sought when a company wants to complete an acquisition for an asset but doesn't have enough liquid capital to do so. The company may be able to get more favorable terms on an acquisition loan because the assets being purchased have a tangible value, as opposed to capital being used to fund daily operations or release a new product line.

Asset Based Lending Loan. An asset based lending loan is a loan that is secured by either residential or commercial real estate, or both, at a fixed percentage of the properties' appraised value. Such a loan is usually limited to a 50% or 65% loan-to-value ratio. For example, for a property valued at $100,000, a lender might provide between $50,000 and $65,000. Sometimes asset based lending programs even allow secondary financing. With asset based lending loans, lenders are assuming considerable risk. Borrowers are more likely to default with this type of loan. In the event of a default resulting in foreclosure, the lender is paid based upon the sale of the assets. If the sale of the asset does not cover the loan, the borrower will have to cover any additional expenses, including past due interest on the loan, past due property taxes, lawyer's fees and other miscellaneous credit and collection fees associated with foreclosure.

Business Line of Credit. A business line of credit is a line of credit used to finance temporary working capital needs of a borrower — usually accounts receivable and inventory. This type of loan is usually extended for one year and the terms are very flexible based upon the needs of the borrower and the requirements of the lender. The terms will be based upon the business's cash flow, credit profiles and financial ratios. The line of credit will be secured by a lien on the assets of the company. It will be extended to companies with a proven earnings track record, adequate financial rations and moderate credit risk. There are three common types of business lines of credit. The first is a demand line of credit, in which the lender leaves the loan open until the lender calls it due. The second is a revolving line of credit, in which the loan is extended for a predetermined period of time. The third is an asset based line of credit, in which a revolving line of credit formula is used and the loan is secured by residential or commercial properties.

Commercial Loans. This is the most common loan application through a traditional bank. This is a debt-based funding arrangement that a business can set up with a financial institution. Commercial loans may be used to fund large capital expenditures and/or operations that a business may otherwise be unable to afford. The challenge is that most businesses must have three years of positive growth and profit in the profit and loss statements with strong credit, collateral and proof of ability to repay.

Corporate Bond. A debt security issued by a corporation and sold to investors. The backing for the bond is usually the payment ability of the company, which is typically money to be earned from future operations. In some cases, the company's physical assets may be used as collateral for bonds. Corporate bonds are considered higher risk than government bonds. As a result, interest rates are almost always higher, even for top-flight credit quality companies. Corporate bonds are issued in blocks of $1,000 in par value, and almost all have a standard coupon payment structure. Corporate bonds may also have call provisions to allow for early prepayment if prevailing rates change.

Equipment Financing. Equipment financing loans are used to purchase equipment, with the equipment used as the collateral on the loan. Equipment financing is generally easier to obtain than general lines of credit, simply because the equipment bought serves as direct collateral for the loan. It's also less risky, in that if a company is unable to make payments, there is no lien against the entire business or the owner's personal real estate: all that is lost is the equipment bought. Depending on the size of the business, equipment financing can cover huge expenses into the millions of dollars.

Another option is an equipment sale-lease back. If a business has existing equipment, it sells the owned equipment and then leases it back from the lender to the company. Essentially the business gets cash for the equipment and maintains use of the equipment. Equipment Leasing is an easier way to find financing for a company's equipment needs and obtain tax benefits at the same time.

Line of Credit. Lines of credit are more general business loans that are often set up to insure against cash flow problems. Instead of getting a check for the full amount of the loan, the financial institution allows a company to borrow up to a certain amount per year - it take out the money in increments as needed. The flexibility comes at a cost, though: if the loan balances is not repaid fairly quickly, lines of credit can quickly become more expensive than other types of loans. A line of credit should be avoided for significant business improvements. They're designed for temporary cash shortfalls.

There are three basic types of lines of credit including "committed" and "revocable" and "Stand-by." Committed Credit Lines are a monetary spending loan balance offered by a financial institution that cannot be suspended without notifying the borrower. A committed credit line is a legal agreement between the financial institution and the borrower outlining the conditions of the credit line. Once signed, the agreement requires the financial institution to lend money to the borrower, provided that the borrower does not break the conditions. Lenders may require the borrower to pay a fee based on the amount that can be borrowed.

Committed credit lines differ from uncommitted credit lines in that they legally bind the lender to provide the funds, rather than giving the lender the option of suspending or canceling the credit line based on market conditions.

Revocable Lines Of Credit are a source of credit provided to an individual or business by a bank or financial institution, which can be revoked or annulled at the lender's discretion or under specific circumstances. A bank or financial institution may revoke a line of credit if the customer's financial circumstances deteriorate markedly, or if market conditions turn so adverse as to warrant revocation, such as in the aftermath of the 2008 global credit crisis. A revocable line of credit can be unsecured or secured, with the former generally carrying a higher rate of interest than the latter.

Standby Lines of Credit are a sum of money, not to exceed a predetermined amount, that can be borrowed in part or in full from a credit granting institution if the borrower needs it. In contrast, an outright loan would be a lump sum of money that the borrower intended to use for certain. A business might establish a standby line of credit with a financial institution in situations where the business needed to guarantee its ability to pay a certain amount of money to a client if the business fails to fully perform on a contract. In this situation, the standby line of credit would act as a performance bond. The standby line of credit might be used as a backup source of funding in case the primary source fails

SBA Business Loan. These are loans to small businesses from private-sector lenders which are guaranteed by the SBA. The SBA has no funds for direct lending. The Certified Development Corporations (CDC's) work with the SBA and private-sector lenders to provide the financing. Because there are many types of SBA loans, knowing which to apply for is vital. The SBA has a strict format for business plans. Five sections are a must, with heavy emphasis on the financials and marketing plan. The ability to repay the loan is also a major focus, along with the credit worthiness of the requestor. SBA loans are most often approved when there is significant collateral available and the requestor has a long term exit strategy. If the requestor's business will make a large positive impact on community development, job creation and construction, the loan is more likely to be approved.

7(a) SBA Small Business Loan. The basic 7(a) loan is the SBA's most flexible business loan program. Loans can be approved for a variety of general business purposes, including working capital, machinery and equipment, furniture and fixtures, land and building, leasehold improvements, and in some cases debt refinancing. Loan terms are available for up to ten years for working capital and up to 25 years for fixed assets. Its name comes from *Section 7(a)* of the *Small Business Act*, which authorizes the Agency to provide business loans to American small businesses.

The SBA does not fully guaranty 7(a) loans. The lender and SBA share the risk that a borrower will not be able to repay the loan in full. The guaranty is a guaranty against payment default. It does not cover imprudent decisions by the lender or misrepresentation by the borrower. A key concept of the 7(a) guaranty loan program is that the loan actually comes from a commercial lender, not the government.

106

The SBA's 7(a) loan program's maximum loan amounts change from time to time. As of this writing, the maximum is $2 million dollars. The SBA's maximum exposure is $1.5 million. Therefore, if a business receives an SBA guaranteed loan for $2 million, the maximum guaranty to the lender will be $1.5 million or 75 percent. There are guarantee fees to be paid, pre-payment penalties and other issues to consider when speaking with an SBA lender.

SBA CDC/504 Program. The CDC/504 loan program is a long-term financing tool, designed to encourage economic development within a community. The 504 program accomplishes this by providing small businesses with long-term, fixed-rate financing to acquire major fixed assets for expansion or modernization.

A Certified Development Company (CDC) is a private, nonprofit corporation which is set up to contribute to economic development within its community. CDCs work with SBA and private sector lenders to provide financing to small businesses, which accomplishes the goal of community economic development. Typically, a CDC/504 project includes: (1) A loan secured from a private sector lender with a senior lien covering up to 50 percent of the project cost; (2) A loan secured from a CDC (backed by a 100 percent SBA-guaranteed debenture) with a junior lien covering up to 40 percent of the project cost; (3) A contribution from the borrower of at least 10 percent of the project cost (equity); (4) This type of setup means that 100% of the project cost is covered either by contribution of equity by the borrower, or the senior or junior lien.

Proceeds from 504 loans must be used for fixed asset projects, such as: (1) The purchase of land, including existing buildings; (2) The purchase of improvements, including grading, street improvements, utilities, parking lots and landscaping; (3) The construction of new facilities or modernizing, renovating or converting existing facilities; (4) The purchase of long-term machinery and equipment.

To be eligible for a CDC/504 loan, the business must be operated for profit and fall within the size standards set by the SBA. Under the 504 Program, a business qualifies as small if it does not have a tangible net worth in excess of $7.5 million and does not have an average net income in excess of $2.5 million after taxes for the preceding two years. Loans cannot be made to businesses engaged in speculation or investment in rental real estate. The maximum SBA debenture is $1.5 million when meeting the job creation criteria or a community development goal. Generally, the business must create or retain one job for every $65,000 provided by the SBA, except for small manufacturers which have a $100,000 job creation or retention goal.

SBA Additional Programs. The SBA offers other programs as well. They include the Patriot Express which has a maximum loan amount of $500,000. In order to be eligible, the business must be owned (at least 51 percent) by a Veteran, Active Duty Military potential retiree within 24 months of separation and discharging Active Duty member within 12 months of discharge (TAP eligible), Reservist and National Guard Current spouse of above or spouse of service member or veteran who died of a service-connected disability. The SBA also offers what's called a "SBA Express" and SBA Community loans. The maximum loan amounts are small but with less paperwork.

Short Term Loans. Short term loans are almost always set up for terms of one year or less, and are repaid in a lump sum at the end of the term, instead of monthly. They're usually for smaller amounts - less than $100,000 - and are best for seasonal inventory buildup or small investments with quick returns.

Small Business Investment Company (SBIC). SBIC is a private lending company which is licensed and regulated by the Small Business Administration (SBA). SBIC's offer venture capital financing to higher-risk small businesses, and SBIC loans are guaranteed by the SBA. SBICs use a combination of funds raised from private sources and money raised through the use of SBA guarantees to make equity and mezzanine capital investments in small businesses. There are approximately 338 SBICs with $17.4 billion in capital in the United States.

Equity Financing

'Equity's' meaning depends very much on the context. In finance, generally, equity is ownership in any asset after all debts associated with that asset are paid off. For example, a car or house with no outstanding debt is considered the owner's equity because he or she can readily sell the item for cash. Stocks are equity because they represent ownership in a company.

Private Securities Overview. Private equity is money invested in firms which have not 'gone public' and therefore are not listed on any stock exchange such as "Over the Counter", "Pink Slips", NASDAQ or the NYSE. Private equity is illiquid because sellers of private stocks (called private securities) must first locate willing buyers. Investors in private equity are generally compensated when: (1) the firm goes public, (2) it is sold or merges with another firm, or (3) it is recapitalized.

Before deciding to seek investors, know the type of investor needed and then research the individuals or investment groups to find those interested in the industry or business. Then include their requirements in opportunity presentation. In general, equity investors require a much more detailed business plan than a plan designed for debt.

Depending on several factors, the Securities Exchange Commission (SEC) may require documentation, circulars, disclosures, and other forms and documents such as a Private Placement Memorandum (PPM).

To summarize, when a business is considering its options for gaining access to capital, it must decide between debt and equity. If equity is the choice, the next decision is whether to raise capital through registered or unregistered securities. These are very murky waters for the uninitiated and counsel should be sought before proceeding to raise capital in this way.

The following equity programs are outlined in alphabetical order and include both finance options and popular terms in the equity finance community.

Accredited investor. "Accredited investor" is a term used by the Securities and Exchange Commission (SEC) under Regulation D to refer to investors who are financially sophisticated and have a reduced need for the protection provided by certain government filings. In order for an individual to qualify as an accredited investor, he or she must accomplish at least one of the following: (1) Earn an individual income of more than $200,000 per year, or a joint income of $300,000, in each of the last two years and expect to maintain the same level of income; (2) Have a net worth exceeding $1 million, either individually or jointly with a spouse; (3) Be a general partner, executive officer, director or a related combination thereof for the issuer of a security being offered.

All-or-None. There are two variations of the best-efforts underwriting: all-or-none or mini-max (discussed below). An all-or-none underwriting requires that the entire issue be sold within a specified time, or else the program is terminated. SEC Rule 15c2-4 requires that all money collected from any sales be deposited in a separate escrow account at an independent bank for the benefit of the investors. If the sale is canceled, then the money must be returned to the investors, and no more orders will be taken; if the underwriting is successful, then most of the money goes to the issuer minus the fees paid to the underwriters.

Alphabet Rounds. The early rounds of funding for a startup company, which get their name because the first is known as "Series A" financing, followed by "Series B" financing, and so on. Alphabet rounds of financing are provided by early investors and venture capital (VC) firms, which are willing to invest in companies with limited operational histories on the hope of larger future gains. These investors will typically wait until the startup has shown some basic signs of maturity and has exhausted its initial seed capital.

Angel Investors. This is a long-term growth plan which emphasizes long-term investments for research, product development and testing. Typically, the product/service(s) are still in the idea phase. For investing at such an early stage of development, Angel Investors have options to receive a large share of ownership in the company.

Authorized Shares. Authorized shares refer to the largest number of shares that a single corporation can issue. The number of authorized shares per company is assessed at the company's creation and can only be increased and decreased through a vote by the shareholders. If at the time of incorporation the documents state that 100 shares are authorized, then only 100 shares can be issued.

Common Stock. Common stock represents ownership in a company and a claim (dividends) on a portion of profits. Investors get one vote per share to elect the board members, who oversee the major decisions made by management. Over the long term, common stock, by means of capital growth, yields higher returns than almost every other investment. This higher return comes at a cost since common stocks entail the most risk. If a company goes bankrupt and liquidates, the common shareholders will not receive money until the creditors, bondholders and preferred shareholders are paid.

Dilution. Dilution is a reduction in earnings per share of common stock that occurs through the issuance of additional shares or the conversion of convertible securities.

Firm Commitment. If the investment bank and company reach an agreement to do an underwriting—also known as a firm commitment—then the investment bank will buy the new securities for an agreed price, and resell the securities to the public at a markup, bearing all of the expenses associated with the sale.

Hedge Funds. Hedge funds are often unregistered because of exemptions related to the *Investment Company Act of 1940*. Most notably is the rule that a hedge fund must have fewer than one hundred investors who are all considered "accredited investors." Additionally, a hedge fund is exempted from registration if all of the fund's investors (no limit to the number) are considered "qualified" investors. To stay "compliant," hedge funds are often set up as private investment partnerships that are open to a limited number of investors and require a very large initial minimum investment. While mutual funds and hedge funds generally perform the same functions, mutual funds are registered with the SEC and hedge funds (generally) are not.

Initial Public Offering – (IPO). An IPO is the first sale of stock by a private company to the public. IPOs are often issued by smaller, younger companies seeking the capital to expand, but can also be done by large privately owned companies looking to become publicly traded. In an IPO, the issuer obtains the assistance of an underwriting firm, which helps it determine what type of security to issue (common or preferred), the best offering price and the time to bring it to market. IPOs can be a risky investment. For the individual investor, it is tough to predict what the stock will do on its initial day of trading and in the near future because there is often little historical data with which to analyze the company. Also, most IPOs are of companies going through a transitory growth period, which are subject to additional uncertainty regarding their future values.

Mini-Max. In this type of offering, a minimum goal and a maximum goal of funds is set to be raised. This gives investors an idea of what will happen if the company does not hit its maximum goal. A mini-max fundraises will normally have an offering that looks like this: the idea of the mini-max fundraises is that the company can get started as long as it achieves its minimum fund raising goal. The company may not spend any of the cash invested until the minimum is achieved (this is often money put into an escrow account until the minimum is raised). In the event the company does not achieve its minimum, the funds are refunded to the investors.

Outstanding Shares. Not to be confused with authorized shares, outstanding shares refer to the number of stocks that a company actually has issued. This number represents all the shares that can be bought and sold by the public as well as all the restricted shares that require special permission before being transacted.

Over-The-Counter. A security traded in some context other than on a formal exchange such as the NYSE, TSX, AMEX, etc. The phrase "over-the-counter" (OTC) (also known as "unlisted stock") can be used to refer to stocks that trade via a dealer network as opposed to on a centralized exchange. It also refers to debt securities and other financial instruments such as derivatives, which are traded through a dealer network. In general, the reason a stock is traded over-the-counter is usually because the company is small, making it unable to meet exchange listing requirements. Be very wary of some OTC stocks, however. The OTCBB stocks are either penny stocks or are offered by companies with bad credit records.

Although NASDAQ operates as a dealer network, NASDAQ stocks are generally not classified as OTC because the NASDAQ is considered a stock exchange. As such, OTC stocks are generally unlisted stocks which trade on the Over the Counter Bulletin Board (OTCBB) or on the pink sheets.

Instruments such as bonds do not trade on a formal exchange and are, therefore, also considered OTC securities. Most debt instruments are traded by investment banks making markets for specific issues. If an investor wants to buy or sell a bond, he or she must call the bank that makes the market in that bond and ask for quotes.

Pink Sheets. A daily publication compiled by the National Quotation Bureau with bid and asks prices of over-the-counter (OTC) stocks, including the market makers who trade them. Unlike companies on a stock exchange, companies quoted on the pink sheets system do not need to meet minimum requirements or file with the SEC. Pink sheets also refers to OTC trading. The pink sheets got their name because they were actually printed on pink paper.

Whether a company trades on the pink sheets can be identified by the stock symbol ending in ".PK".

Preferred Stock. Preferred stock represents some degree of ownership in a company but usually doesn't come with the same voting rights. (This may vary depending on the company.) With preferred shares, investors are usually guaranteed a fixed dividend forever. This is different than common stock, which has variable dividends that are never guaranteed. Another advantage is that in the event of liquidation, preferred shareholders are paid off before the common shareholder (but still after debt holders). Preferred stock may also be callable, meaning that the company has the option to purchase the shares from shareholders at anytime for any reason (usually for a premium).

Private Equity. Private equity is equity capital that is not quoted on a public exchange. Private equity consists of investors and funds that make investments directly into private companies or conduct buyouts of public companies that result in a delisting of public equity. Capital for private equity is raised from retail and institutional investors, and can be used to fund new technologies, expand working capital within an owned company, make acquisitions, or to strengthen a balance sheet.

The size of the private equity market has grown steadily since the 1970s. The majority of private equity consists of institutional investors and accredited investors who can commit large sums of money for long periods of time. Private equity investments often demand long holding periods to allow for a turnaround of a distressed company or a liquidity event such as an IPO or sale to a public company.

Private equity firms will sometimes pool funds together to take very large public companies private. Many private equity firms conduct what are known as leveraged buyouts (LBOs), where large amounts of debt are issued to fund a large purchase. Private equity firms will then try to improve the financial results and prospects of the company in the hope of reselling the company to another firm or cashing out via an IPO.

Private Investment in Public Equity (PIPE). A PIPE is a private investment firm's, mutual fund's or other qualified investors' purchase of stock in a company at a discount to the current market value per share for the purpose of raising capital.

There are two main types of PIPEs - traditional and structured. A traditional PIPE is one in which stock, either common or preferred, is issued at a set price to raise capital for the issuer. A structured PIPE, on the other hand, issues convertible debt (common or preferred shares). This financing technique is popular due to the relative efficiency in time and cost of PIPEs, compared to more traditional forms of financing such as secondary offerings.

In a PIPE offering there are less regulatory issues with the SEC and there is also no need for an expensive road show, lowering both the costs and time it takes to receive capital. PIPEs are great for small- to medium-sized public companies, which have a hard time accessing more traditional forms of equity financing.

Private Placement Memorandum. In preparing for a private placement, the company prepares offering materials containing information about the company and the securities being offered. A Private Placement Memorandum (PPM) is most often created with multiple sections including the offering, risks and disclosures, a business description or business plan, subscription agreements and company operating agreements. In order to sell unregistered securities, the company must produce a PPM which describes the company's intentions (use of funds) and declare its status as an unregistered security. A PPM typically includes: (1) Executive Summary; (2) The Offering (Terms of the offering); (3) Risks & Disclosures; (4) Business Description (Business Plan); (5) Operating Agreement; (6) Subscription Agreement.

Registered Securities. All securities must be registered. Per the Securities Acts of 1933 and 1934, all securities should be "registered" unless they are deemed "exempt." Not only do the securities need to be registered but the agents selling them and the broker/dealers representing the sale should be licensed as well.

Any security that does not have an effective registration statement on file with the SEC is considered "unregistered." To sell or attempt to sell a financial security before it is registered is considered a felony. As stated however, provisions have been made over the years to allow for these "exceptions."

Regulation D. Regulation D contains three rules providing exemptions from the registration requirements, allowing some companies to offer and sell their securities without having to register the securities with the SEC. While companies using a Regulation D exemption do not have to register their securities and usually do not have to file reports with the SEC, they must file what's known as a "Form D" after they first sell their securities. Form D is a brief notice that includes the names and addresses of the company's executive officers and stock promoters, but contains little other information about the company. There are three types of Regulation D Exemptions, 504, 505 and 506.

Rule 504 of Regulation D: (1) Provides an exemption from the registration requirements of the federal securities laws for some companies; (2) Offer and sell up to $1,000,000 of their securities in any 12-month period; (3) Sells exclusively according to state law exemptions that permit general solicitation and advertising; (4) Sells to an unlimited number of "accredited investors" and allows purchases by non-accredited investors; (5) Any information a company provides to investors must be free from false or misleading statements. Similarly, a company should not exclude any information if the omission makes what is provided to investors false or misleading.

A 504 Reg D filing has many "slang terms within the industry including: (1) "Family & Friends" round; (2) or a "Seed;" or (3) a "Series A;" or (4) a first, "Tranche" Round as it is the first of possibly other "rounds." Seed capital often comes from the company founders' personal assets or from friends and family. The amount of money is usually relatively small because the business is still in the idea or conceptual stage. Such a venture is generally at a pre-revenue stage and seed capital is needed for research and development, to cover initial operating expenses until a product or service can start generating revenue, and to attract the attention of venture capitalists.

Rule 505 of Regulation D: (1) Can only offer and sell up to $5 million of its securities in any 12-month period; (2) May sell to an unlimited number of "accredited investors" and up to 35 other persons who do not need to satisfy the sophistication or wealth standards associated with other exemptions; (3) Must inform purchasers that they receive "restricted" securities, meaning that the securities cannot be sold for six months or longer without registering them; and (4) Cannot use general solicitation or advertising to sell the securities.

Rule 506 of Regulation D: (1) Rule 506 of Regulation D is considered a "safe harbor" for the private offering exemption of Section 4(2) of the Securities Act; (2) Companies using the Rule 506 exemption can raise an unlimited amount of money; (3) May sell its securities to an unlimited number of "accredited investors" and up to 35 other purchases; (4) Unlike Rule 505, all non-accredited investors, either alone or with a purchaser representative, must be sophisticated—that is, they must have sufficient knowledge and experience in financial and business matters to make them capable of evaluating the merits and risks of the prospective investment; (5) Purchasers receive "restricted" securities, meaning that the securities cannot be sold for at least a year without registering them.

Registration. Before securities, like stocks, bonds and notes can be offered for sale to the public, they first must be registered with the Securities and Exchange Commission (SEC). Any stock that does not have an effective registration statement on file with the SEC is considered "unregistered." To sell or attempt to sell a financial security before it is registered is considered a felony. However, certain exemptions apply. For example, a privately-owned corporation may issue shares of stock to its executives and board members, but the new stockholders must notify the SEC before selling the stock to someone else. In addition, companies can raise capital by soliciting investments from individuals outside the company who are considered to be "qualified investors." The SEC defines a qualified investor as someone who has a net worth of at least one million dollars or an annual income in excess of $200,000. Individuals who meet "qualified investor" status also can become victims of "private offering" unregistered securities scams.

Rule 144. Privately Held Company Rule 144: Per the SEC, "Rule 144 provides an exemption and permits the public resale of restricted or control securities if a number of conditions are met, including how long the securities are held, the way in which they are sold, and the amount that can be sold at any one time. But even if you've met the conditions of the rule, you can't sell your restricted securities to the public until you've gotten a transfer agent to remove the legend." The rules pertaining to #144 should be thoroughly read and examined prior to taking action. This rule mostly pertains to insiders who have gained access to stock and wish to resell it to the public.

Standby Commitment. When the investment bank also has a standby commitment with its client, then the investment bank agrees to purchase any subsequent new issues of stock shares at the subscription price that are not purchased by current stockholders in a rights offering, which it will then sell to the general public as a dealer in the stock. The investment bank takes a risk, however, in that the price of the stock could decline during the two to four weeks of a rights offering.

Tranches. "Tranche" is the French word for "slice". In finance, "tranche" is the technical term for series rounds of the same offerings. The definition is that of a piece, portion or slice of a deal or structured financing. This portion is one of several related securities that are offered at the same time but have different risks, rewards and/or maturities.

Unregistered Securities. The cost of registering a security when going public is enormous. When a company goes public it must file applications, legal and accounting forms, certifications and other costs that can be in the hundreds of thousands of dollars. The Securities and Exchange Commission (SEC) created exemptions for private companies in order to raise capital with unregistered securities. The most common of the programs is called a Regulation "D" filing – sometimes called "Blue-Sky" filing.

120

Venture Capital. Once a product/service is researched, the target market identified and a business plan written, Venture Capital investment may be more appropriate. Not to be confused with an early development project, Venture Capital is typically used for the actual manufacturing, distribution or marketing. Venture Capitalists tend to expect a faster return on investment than an Angel Investor.

Creative Financing

Grants. A grant is an amount of money given, usually by a government or nonprofit organization, to fund certain projects. One may receive a grant for academic or scientific research, or to further one's education, or to engage in charity work. The United States government makes many grants, often of an educational or scientific nature. Grants are also a key part of many philanthropic foundations' activities. In some instances grants are applicable if a business existence will benefit and/or support an organization or group. Typically, grant requests are specific in nature and require a particular format determined by the grantor.

Royalty Financing. Royalty financing is a relatively new concept that offers an alternative to regular debt financing (loans and trade credit) and equity financing (venture capital and stock sales). In a royalty financing arrangement, a small business would receive a specific amount of funds from an investor or group of investors. This money might be put toward launching a new product or expanding the company's marketing efforts. In exchange, the investors would receive a percentage of the company's future revenues over a certain period of time, up to a specific amount. The investment can be considered an "advance" to the company, and the periodic percentage payments can be considered "royalties" to the investors.

Read more:
http://www.answers.com/topic/royalty-
financing#ixzz1XM9WfreU
http://www.sec.gov/answers/regd.htm
http://www.finra.org/Investors/ToolsCalculators/BrokerCheck/
See http://www.sec.gov/answers/rule144.htm.

~ A Hero ~

Our next hero is Mr. George C. Rivera, founder and Chief Executive Officer of Total Resources International Incorporated (TRI) in Walnut, California. *TRI* is one of the nation's leading manufacturers of first aid and emergency survival kits in the United States, producing millions of kits per year. Employing more than 100 people, George started the company with amazingly humble beginnings. 20 years ago in 1991, George was bankrupt, owed family and friends money, and had lost a major sale causing more than a million dollars in losses. Instead of seeing this as a major setback, George saw it as God's greatest blessing upon his life.

It was at this point in his life that George committed his life to Jesus Christ as his Lord and Savior. In one of their bible studies at work, the teacher suggested that George seek the bible, live his life righteously, and run his business according to Matthew 6:33, "But seek first His kingdom and His righteousness, and all these things will be given to you as well." (New International Version ©1984). Since then, by God's grace, George and his executive team have developed an incredible company at *TRI*.

On *TRI's* seven acre facility are the usual buildings – production, shipping, receiving, and corporate headquarters. But George also built a fellowship hall for bible studies and praise and worship.The first 30 minutes of each work day is dedicated to prayer and devotionals. Imagine how inspiring and powerful it is to see all the employees united in oneness, holding hands in one huge prayer circle. They give thanks, praise God, and pray for each other, as well as the company.

Every Monday during lunch, they have men's and women's fellowships – both in English and Spanish. On Wednesdays at lunch, their bilingual bible study is open to everyone – employees, vendors, sales reps, and friends, where they can see George playing the drums in the *TRI* worship band. The crew knows how to have fun too! Throughout the week, it's common to see employees play friendly, yet competitive games of volleyball, soccer, and basketball on the company's full courts. During the consistent 10:00 AM and 3:00 PM mandatory breaks, it's also not unusual to see employees playing pool, air hockey or other recreational games in the break room.

And profits? Oh yes. While most would relish in their company's profitability, George established a non-profit organization called *Vision Himpossible Ministries* in 1996, to which he donates a significant amount of his personal income and the company's income to support missionaries and churches of all nations, who are in the field doing God's work.

It is one thing to see all this in action and hear about it – it is another to personally meet and work with George. He does not only practice what he preaches by applying God's word in the workplace, but he also teaches to all and encourages others to live their lives worthy of God. When a crisis arises at the company, as is the case with every business, rather than reacting on impulse, George and his team will stop, reflect, and pray on the challenge, seeking God's guidance through His word.

At times when most would be discouraged, depressed or give up, George takes refuge and seeks God's word and will for them. I have witnessed this in action, on numerous occasions when only a miracle could fix what would otherwise ruin companies. When a national recall caused operations to be halted, when vendor deliveries were late, when accounts receivable exceeded a million dollars more than 45 days late, they meditated on God's word, lifted it up in prayer, seeking His answers. Through the economy's financial downturn, along with personal trials and tribulations, *TRI* continues to persevere, grow and claim God's victory throughout it all. I want to encourage you to be inspired, learn from this lesson, and build your company with faith and conviction that is unsurpassed, as George has done. With God's grace and mercy upon your life, all things are possible. Believe it. Visit *TRI* any Wednesday at 12:30 to witness how faith and placing a business in God's hand can create true stories that would otherwise be unbelievable.

126

CHAPTER 3
DEVELOPING A BUSINESS PLAN

We have been developing business plans for 17 years. The information included is a result of writing hundreds of them. We have gleaned this template from high volume companies, web-based software, off-the-shelf software, attending business plan writing classes, seminars, college courses and having read more than 1,000 plans. We feel this is a highly comprehensive version which covers just about every section of a plan for multiple purposes. We'll start with the top-10 reasons for a business plan in alphabetical order:

1. Assess feasibility of the model.
2. Attract strategic partners.
3. Attract investors.
4. Determine capital needs.
5. Develop the revenue model.
6. Develop operations management.
7. Establish and research assumptions.
8. Evaluate the market.
9. Position the brand and marketing plan.
10. Reduce risk.

Developing a professional-grade business plan is complicated, time consuming and sometimes seems arcane, especially to the entrepreneur who just wants to "get on with it." However, for the serious business owner a business plan is essential. Here are a few reasons why.

First, developing a business plan forces the entrepreneur to take a hard look at the overall industry. Understanding the market, trends, maturity, market share and long term planning are all essential pieces to the puzzle.

Second, is a focus on the Company. While the first reason focuses on the industry, the Company fit into the industry is key to success. By writing a plan, the company starts taking shape on paper. This includes capabilities, resources, strengths and weaknesses, competitive advantage, growth planning, shape sales and operations.

Thirdly, a business plan forces a look at the bottom line. Dissecting the financials including labor costs, goods and all ongoing expenses in advance saves time and money. Knowing the breakeven point, switch point, and profitability pushes a model into reality!

Finally, developing a business plan equips the entrepreneur with options in case things don't go as well, or go better than expected. A quality business plan is like a road map. It points the readers in the direction, gives benchmarks to measure success and lays out alternate routes. A business plan is not magic and it's no guarantee of success. A business plan works just like anything else: Put the effort into it to make it good, and it moves the chance for success further up the ladder.

Eight Types of Business Plans. A business plan is essential to apply for a capital of all types. Every new or expanding business needs capital to operate. There are eight types of business plans which fit different financial needs. When writing the plan, keep in mind the purpose and write accordingly.

Strategic and tactical plan. Strategic and Tactical business planning is for the business owner who intends his/her business to be profitable and strong, regardless of funding objectives. (Strategic and Tactical business plans are not used for loan approvals.) A Strategic and Tactical plan will focus on the product/service(s), cash flow, marketing and distribution. It has a strong exit strategy for the owners.

Personal Loan/Investment. When asking family and friends to invest in a business, it's always a good idea to give them a business plan. Issues of credit and experience are less important than the repayment schedule and timelines. Remember, however, that even family and friends should be provided formal documentation when providing capital.

Early-stage/Seed/angel financing. This is a long-term growth plan which emphasizes long-term investments for research, product development and testing. This is often referred to as the "proof of concept" phase. Typically, the product/service(s) are still in the idea phase. For investing at such an early stage of development, angel investors receive a large share of ownership in the company.

Venture capital and investment banking. Once a product/service is researched, the target market identified, post revenue, post proof of concept stage, venture capital investment may be more appropriate. Not to be confused with an early development project, venture capital is typically used for dealing with economies of scale, large scale manufacturing development, distribution or marketing. Also, the return on investment occurs sooner than an angel investment.

Conventional bank loan. Many requirements must be met for a bank loan approval, including a detailed business plan focusing on the ability to repay the loan and on the requestor's creditworthiness. Typically, new businesses do not qualify because of the need to show a two-year financial track record.

SBA guaranteed loan. Because there are many types of SBA loans, knowing which to apply for is vital. The SBA has a strict format for business plans. Five sections are a must, with heavy emphasis on the financials and marketing plan. The ability to repay the loan is also a major focus, along with the credit worthiness of the requestor. SBA loans are most often approved when there is significant collateral available and the requestor has a long term exit strategy. If the requestor's business will make a large positive impact on community development, job creation and construction, the loan is more likely to be approved.

Grants. In some instances grants may be applicable if a business' existence will benefit and/or support an organization or group. Typically, grant requests are specific in nature and require a particular format determined by the grantor.

Marketing Plans. A marketing plan focuses on the product's ability to get into the market and be sold. It will generalize on the issues of production, operations, management, manufacturing and distribution. However, it will give a detailed analysis of the potential market, industry buying trends, niche, market penetration tables, advertising and branding as well as specific examples of the items to be used.

Appearances may be important. A business plan's design and aesthetic appeal are as important as what is in it. The business plan is the "calling card" or "business introduction" to a potential capital provider. If it's unorganized, haphazardly written or looks like it's been cut and pasted together, it sends a negative message regarding the writer's professionalism. A further complication is that there is no "industry standard" way of writing a business plan. However, most business plan forms, templates or outlines generally contain the same topical material arranged in different ways. Here are some helpful hints to make a business plan look as professional as, hopefully, the content is.

First, let's deal with aesthetics. When writing a business plan, follow a clear outline and have a consistent numbering system and formatting throughout. Depending on the length, a table of contents accurately reflects the topical divisions as well as the correct page numbers. The text alignment formatting needs to be consistent throughout (usually "justified" is best, meaning the body text extends from margin to margin). Major headings need to be in a larger font and "bolded" while sub-headings should simply be "bolded." Make sure any included pictures help explain the text. Maps, pictures of property, interior and exterior shots of the place of business, blueprints, architectural renderings, product shots and headshots of the key owners or management team are appropriate, but need to be well placed and not overwhelm the text.

Second, let's deal with the topical content itself. After a business plan is written, a cover letter may need to be included. The cover letter should include the purpose of the business plan and summarize the business and financial models, how much capital is required and an explanation why the capital provider should invest. This letter is sent with the business plan and is placed in front.

Writing a business plan with these guidelines in mind will improve both the professional appearance and content of the presentation.

Work with a professional. A business owner should be prepared to add content to the business plan. When possible, the owner should write as much of a plan as possible. But for many reasons, it is not always applicable, practical or possible. While it is assumed an entrepreneur has experience in his/her chosen field, most business owners are not experts in marketing, accounting, research, industry trends, operational planning, staffing or competition. The best plans tend to be written when an entrepreneur and a professional work together.

An experienced business plan writer takes the business owner's ideas and turns them into a profitable enterprise. A planner will formulate proper ratios of marketing, advertising budgets and inventory levels. An experienced planner will research the competition to help make strategic decisions about market share, industry trends and ultimately, financing.

Once the plan is written, it becomes a matter of implementation. Some writers will assist in the implementation of the plan and others will not. Be sure to know from the beginning if the business plan writer will assist in the implementation process. Lastly, a business plan should constantly be reviewed and updated, as necessary throughout the life of the business. Times will change, and so should the business plan.

In the Los Angeles area, business plan writers' prices range from $35 to $275 per hour. A professionally completed plan will range in cost between $2,500 and $25,000. The cost variation is typically based on the amount of input provided by the entrepreneur and the experience of the business plan writer. The amount of research and validation of all claims is the largest distinguisher when comparing price and professionalism. While anyone can purchase *Business Plan Pro* by PaloAlto Software for $100 to $200, the challenge is not the template but the input and validation of the claims.

What follows in this chapter is a business plan template outline that is easy to follow. Each section and sub-section heading is in bold type. Under each sub-section is a description of information or questions needed to answer which defines what needs to go there. To provide some of that information, please refer to *Chapter One – The 125 Steps for Launching a Business.* There the reader can find many resources to help locate the information needed. When the business plan is completed it should have a cover page (not included here) which includes a company logo, the company title, the company's web site (if available or known) the company principal's name and title (owner, CEO, President, etc.) with contact information (the company address, phone number and email).

Statement of purpose. This is a one-page document written to gain the reader's interest and trust. It should include the purpose of the plan, a very brief business model, financial model, use of funds and a summary. The statement of purpose differs from an executive summary as it is used as a marketing tool to get parties interested in the business quickly and effectively. The information in the statement of purpose should also serve double-duty as a cover letter to capital providers. This is the last part of the business plan to write. To help simplify the process, cut and paste the greatest parts of the plan and then revise and rewrite into a summary format.

Purpose of the Business Plan. What is the main purpose of writing the business plan (clarity of the business model, clarity of the financial model, organizational planning, funding, attracting a management team or a combination of these)? Get to the point quickly. The purpose should focus on the need for money. State how much is needed. Include whether seeking financing through a debt deal or equity deal. (This should all be written in the first sentence.) The second sentence should be more specific: an SBA loan, from venture capitalists, etc.

Business Model. What niche is being filled? What problem is being solved by this company's model? How does the company plan to fulfill the issue? The business model should include the industry and sector of the business and the number of products or services the business earns revenue from.

Financial Model. How will the company make money? What are the financial projections? What is the profit from products or services offered? What are the major costs? What is the overhead, payroll, supplies, etc.? What is the proposed return on investment (ROI) and time by putting the model into practice? If it is for a loan, how will it be paid back?

Capital Required and Use of Funds. Company XXX has accomplished the following major milestones. To hit future objectives and milestones, it needs $XXX to achieve these objectives. Opportunities are present for XXX Company by achieving these milestones. Break down the funds more specifically into categories that tell the lender or investor how the capital will be used.

Summary. Explain why the investor/banker should provide capital to the company. Remember, the summary needs to sell the owner. Write it to generate a desire to invest. Talk about the great idea and the stage of development. Include the strengths of the ownership and/or the management team being assembled. Also include a call to action (what is the reader to do?) and the contact information for the person who can give him more information. The summary can sell the owner – summarize his business accomplishments and successes. If the owner doesn't have a strong business success background, then sell the business. Talk about the great idea the business represents, and the stage of development.

Section 1 – The Executive Summary. The executive summary should be written last. Think of it as a five minute interview that is two to three pages. It is a scaled-down version of the entire plan written as a summary of the entire document. It should be written in about seven paragraphs as shown and so that it may be extracted from the plan to become a stand-alone document for capital providers: investors, bankers or other readers who may not take the time to read the plan in its entirety. When sending the executive summary as a stand-alone document, it should include a cover letter which is written using the information from the statement of purpose. Again, it's recommended to cut and paste from pertinent sections of the document and then rewrite them. It should take about 30 minutes if the plan is written properly.

Business Profile. This shall include a brief history of the who, what, when, where, how and why of the business, including major milestones achieved. Remember, this section has to have "everything" in it because many bankers often do not read past this paragraph. Provide justification for this particular location rather than other cities.

The Product or Service. A brief summary of what niche is being filled or what problem is being resolved by this company. As one client puts it, "What is the special sauce?" What sources (sourcing) is used to gain the raw materials. What part of the delivery process does this company provide (manufacturing, distribution, wholesale, retail, etc.). Always separate product from service. If the company offers both, talk about each one separately. Never say "as necessary" – the purpose of the plan is to show knowledge of what is necessary. End with something strong about the product or service.

Marketing Strategy. The "four P's" (Product, Placement, Promotion and Price) as well as a brief summary of the target market, the market potential, a brief analysis of the marketing mix, branding plan, advertising plan, customer retention management plan and the marketing budget. A brief overview of competitors should be included as well. First sentence needs to say what the strategy is. Talk about the benchmark that should be set before decreasing the marketing plan. Example: "Marketing budget shall not decrease until the second year revenue goals have been achieved as outlined in Section 5 of this business plan."

Financial Objectives. How much money is needed to hit major milestones? Breakdown the use of funds specifically. Include use of funds, overhead, payroll, supplies, etc.. Also include revenue sources and projected revenue for two to three years.

Management and operations. Discuss management team's qualifications and years of experience. Be able to verify all claims. Cover the major milestones such as facilities, hours of operation, staff needs, etc.

Exit Strategy. The exit strategy is one of the most important paragraphs outside of the repayment to the capital acquired through debt or equity. The lender/investor wants assurance that he will get paid. Assuming all milestones are achieved, what is the exit strategy of the current team (i.e. to sell to another company, to merge with another company, to acquire other companies, to go public, to close on a pre-determined date for a specific reason)? If the current team intends to keep the company, what plans are in place to grow the company to the next level? What will happen to the company in the event of death or disability of the key personnel?

Executive Summary final paragraph. Write a summary that makes the reader take action, whether that means ordering a full copy of the business plan or meeting with the applicant in person, fill out a loan package or apply for a capital injection application for Venture or Angel investment entities. Again, include contact information for the person who can provide more information about the business or provide the business plan. Make this a summary of benchmarks and milestones. For example, "With the capital injection of $1.5 million required by this plan, [the company] will be the premier ..." Be clear about what is going on: "[The company] will grow..." "One of the most important benchmarks [the company] intends to achieve is..." When talking about money, talk about profit and profit margin. Be realistic about the time frame. For example, "While the economy sagged in 2008, a significant aspect of this plan is that acquisition and build out of the locations will occur during economic rebound."

Section 2 – Business Description – Overview. Simply, what kind of business is it? How did it get started (historical background) What customers needs are satisfied? What value will the company have to its customers? What is the company providing in society that has not already been implemented? What major milestones have been achieved? Provide a vision of an opportunity to make a profit. Talk about Supply/Demand factors. Do not rehash the products and services the company offers. Those will be covered in Section 3. An example of a company overview would be, "[The Company], a privately held LLC is a hospitality company providing a unique entertainment experience to communities which need and can support such a venue." When the company or the entrepreneur does not have history, then writing skills need to be creative and emphasize the opportunity.

Mission Statement. In 35 words or less, explain the business's reason for being and explain the guiding principles including who, what, when, where, how and why. The mission statement should be able to explain the entire business if it were being read to someone (for example a banker). And it's very important to include the company name. Note: The Mission Statement should identify: Who is the target market? Who are we serving? How is the market being served by this company? Where is it being served? If it's possible to include the company's sustainable competitive advantage in the mission statement, add it here.

Company Goals and Objectives. State specific sales objectives. For example, between now to end of next year, what will be accomplished? Should be a chart (Ex: Microsoft Project) with dates across the top, and benchmarks throughout to show where and when they occur.

Business Model. What is driving the market to want this product or service? (This may be government, consumer trends, popularity, necessity, wants, political, economic, etc.). What is the client introducing to the market? Talk about the industry and sector the company operates in.

Business Entity options. They include:
1. "C" Corporation;
2. "S" Corporation;
3. Limited Liability Company (LLC);
4. Limited Liability Partnership (LLP);
5. Partnership;
6. Sole Proprietorship;
7. Foreign Corporation;
8. Other.

DBA Name (Doing Business As) filing. The business normally does business under an assumed name unless it is a corporation doing business under its legal name. For example, if John Jones is doing business as "Happy Cleaners", then a DBA filing is necessary. If a corporation is doing business under a name other than its corporation name (such as "ABC Corporation DBA Happy Cleaners"), then a DBA is needed. Also provide information that shows that the business name has been applied for.

SIC Code (Standard Industrial Classification code). SIC codes are important for business industry searches, insurance quotes and workers compensation estimates. SIC codes affect the financial forecasts because some businesses are more risky than others – more risky to finance and/or more risky to insure. However some SIC codes are not always up to date, so include NAICS codes (North American Industrial Classification Codes) which is a more flexible and modern system.

Ownership. A percentage of ownership – list all owners with 10% ownership or more, listed in order of most ownership to least. Make sure this is consistent with what has already been talked about in the plan.

Contact information. Include business Address and/or Mailing Address. Business phone numbers

Tax Identification Number. An Employer's tax Identification Number (EIN) may be obtained by going to www.irs.gov. Search the forms section for an online EIN request. A qualified attorney or CPA can help.

Resale Number (When Appropriate). This number is assigned by the State Board of Equalization for the collection of sales tax. If a business is collecting sales tax, a "reseller's permit" is required.

Industry Trends. Describe the industry the company operates within. What expected changes will affect the business? How is the company prepared to take advantage of the reported trends? What strengths does the company have that will best serve the trends? Ensure to use credible references. Validate all claims and quotes. When researching an industry, here are some questions to answer: What is the difference between the industry and the market? The industry is the entire field of manufacturers, producers and/or service providers (including competitors). The market is the people who buy the product or service. The industry might be increasing, but is the market going up as well? What are the trends: National trends, state trends, city trends? Is new technology or are new products being introduced to the market? What's happening in the future that may affect the company? What is happening to the industry in general? Growing? Declining? Staying even (leveling)? Is there a lot of consolidation? Who is the "monster" (leading company) in the industry? Who else does the same thing? If the industry changes, is there another market the business can provide products and services to?

Here are some sources for researching the industry the business operates in: Most industries have trade associations so associations are a good place to start. (Ex. National Restaurant Association) Hoovers.com (Some info is only for subscribers). Search engines (ex. "restaurant industry trends").

Section 3 - Product or Service. Define the product or the service or both. Be sure to include all products and/or services, especially those that bring revenue into the

140

company. If multiple products or services are offered, create an overview/description of each one. (This provides a launch point for the financial forecasts created later.)

New or Improved. Is it a new Product to Market or an improvement of an existing product or service?

Stage of Development. What is the current stage of development for the product or service? Is the product a fully developed product or is it in development now? Is testing completed? Is Market Research completed? Is it ready for mass production pending capital? Is it ready for marketing pending capital? Is it ready for manufacturing pending capital? Is it ready for Distribution pending capital?

Intellectual Property Owned by the Company. Includes trademarks, patents and/or technological advances owned by the company. Note: An intellectual property attorney should be consulted, if one has not been already, if the company has, or intends to have, trademarks or patents filed.

Pricing Strategy. What is the financial model of the product or service? How much is being charged to the customer and how much did it cost to produce the product or service. Why the product or service priced this way? Building the pricing strategy and identifying what the product/services cost helps to negotiate pricing with a broker or retailer – the company can document how much it costs to produce each product and/or provide each service.

Special Situations. Does the product or service require special machining, molds or other high cost of goods?

Licensing. Are special licenses required to operate the business? If so, what are they? Does the company already have them?

Competitive Advantages - Features and Benefits. What are the major competitive advantages of the product or service over the direct and indirect competition?

Photos/Drawings/Examples. Keep to a minimum in this section; place most in the Supporting Documents section.

Section 4 - Marketing Plan. A business owner needs to plan and budget for marketing because almost every failed business didn't plan for or spend the right amount of money on a marketing plan. That's why this section is one of the most important in the entire plan. A general rule of thumb for a marketing budget is to set aside 10% of revenue (or initial capital) if the company's annual revenue (or initial capital) is five million dollars or less. However, the minimum to set aside under any business circumstance is 7% and the maximum is 12%.

Be sure to have clearly identified the target market before writing the marketing plan. Remember, the end-user is not necessarily the person being marketed to. Think of baby food as an example. The end-user is the baby. However, the person who writes the check is the parent. The parent therefore is who the company markets to! Spend marketing dollars on the target market as much as possible. These are the dollars that will have an impact.

Here are some other questions to consider before writing this section:
1. The number one question is what is the market driver (i.e. what makes people buy this product or service)?
2. How is the product or service different from the competitors?
3. How much money does the company have to invest to get a person to spend money for the product/service? How much does it cost per client per year? This

helps determine wasted marketing money. What is the cost per $1,000 spent on marketing? Typically this cost can be from the .10 to 1.00 range. What is the cost for exposure? What is the cost per new customer?

The marketing plan and budget are forecasts and must make financial sense. See Chapter 4 for the compete outline of a marketing plan. In summary, the sections included in a marketing plan are:
1. Marketing Overview (Situation Analysis);
2. Marketing Strategy;
3. Primary Target Market;
4. Demographics;
5. Primary Market Research;
6. Stakeholders, Strategic Alliances, and Collaborators;
7. Secondary Market Research;
8. Competitive Analysis;
9. Direct Competition;
10. Competition chart;
11. Indirect Competitive Factors;
12. Sustainable Competitive Advantage;
13. Market Size, Market Share, Market Penetration;
14. Barriers to Entry;
15. SWOT Analysis;
16. Product Placement, Promotion, & Price;
17. Web site;
18. Advertising Budget;
19. Branding/Graphic Imagery;
20. Customer Retention Management (CRM) & Social media;
21. Sales Cycle;
22. Grass Roots Campaign;
23. Public Relations;
24. Implementation & Control;
25. Timing;

26. Contingency Planning.

Section 5 - Overview of the Financial Plan. Provide an overview of the financial model, historical data and capital required as well as forecast information and the nuts/bolts of the cash flow plan. What research was used to substantiate claims of growth? What is the plan to finance ongoing operations? Does the business need lines of credit, or accounts receivable loans or other financing methods particular to the company? This should all be discussed in the overview. If past financials are available, use them as a basis for this section. Create historical records optimally for three years.

Financial Performance Review (historical review). If this is for an ongoing business then a historical review of the finances should be placed here. This includes a three-year trend of revenue and profitability. (Most banks will require three years – if the business has less, and then provide whatever is available). Tax returns are helpful. *QuickBooks* or other profit and loss statement software printouts pasted here are extremely helpful. A comparison of the performance to industry standards is helpful as well. For instance, if the company is a restaurant business but its cost of goods is only 22% instead of the industry standard of 35%, then that is a good argument that must be explained. Early stage companies obviously won't have much, if any, financial performance.

12-Month Profit and Loss Performance Projection. Provide a spreadsheet which should have a series of assumptions that support the projections. The format should include revenue minus costs of goods/services which provides a gross profit. It should then be followed by fixed, variable, and payroll expenses. By subtracting the gross profit from expenses a net profit emerges.

5-Year Profit and Loss Forecast. The driving force and purpose of a five-year forecast is the growth of revenue and the relationship between growth and expenses. Fixed costs should not increase in the same ratios as the variable costs to increased revenue. A key aspect of the five year forecast is the research used which predicts the growth potential. The first year should be a summary of the 12-month forecast. Subsequent years should show a reasonable, conservative growth rate based on solid data substantiating the claims. The 5 Year Profit and Loss Forecast is the single most important page - every banker will spend time reading it. It needs to match 12 month forecast. The hard part is justifying projections of growth: what assumption is made to show growth, and based on what?

Cash Flow Forecast. The point of this worksheet is to plan how much the business needs before start-up, for preliminary expenses, operating expenses and reserves. Continue to update it and using it after start-up. It will enable the management to foresee shortages in time to do something about them - perhaps cut expenses or perhaps negotiate a loan. The cash flow projection is just a forward look at the company's checking account. A cash flow statement will show whether the working capital is adequate. If the projected cash balance ever goes negative, the company will need more start-up capital. This plan will also predict just when and how much the start-up needs to borrow.

Financial Model (Break-even Calculation). The financial model should take into account the revenue, minus cost of goods, expenses with a forecasted profit based on a "best-case scenario" that gives the reader a good indication of how the financial model of the business works. It should be simple and to the point without all the details. It should show "0" at the bottom for profit. A break-even analysis predicts the sales volume, at a given price, required to recover total costs. Assumptions used are a key in this report and should be provided immediately following the report. How much product do we need to sell to cover all the costs? What is the overhead? What is payroll? How much sales does company have to do to break even? Account for marketing - how much marketing to make the break even?

Assumptions. Assumptions are explanations with supporting data and research (not guessing). It should be outlined as a "bullet-point" explanation of relevant assumptions for receivables, sales, average day's outstanding, inventory levels, debt levels, assets, reserves and amortization schedules. Provide research that backs up what was calculated. For example, "What says 20% compounded was reasonable?" The Assumptions Worksheet should explain everything: What are the assumptions for cost of goods? Has the company received invoices from vendors? Do the company have bids from vendors?

Capital Requirements. Every reader of the business plan will review this section. It is vitally important that the use of funds is as accurate as possible, without providing pages of individual costs. However, any single item over $1,000 should have its own line-item. Items under $1,000 should be lumped together. Assets to be acquired are important as well as non-asset single purchases, consumables, equipment, marketing expenses and other working capital requirements. For most businesses, contingencies should equal at least 20 percent of the total of all other start-up expenses. It is likely the company will need what is known as "owner equity" - the amount of cash already put into the project by the owner. In the 2008 economy, this is often 30% of the starting operating budget – be prepared. Ensure to include the owner equity and the source of such funds. They may be savings, family seed money, gifts, inheritance, money market accounts, certificates of deposits, or other short term loans against assets. Last, most often benchmarks and milestones with stages of cash expenditures should be outlined as well. The best course of action is to develop six-month benchmarks for cash expenditures. How much will be spent over what time-frame? How many months lose money before positive? Start-up companies will have negative months. Some existing companies will also have negative months.

Section 6 – Ownership. A list of the owners and a brief resume (one paragraph) which substantiates their qualifications and position in the company. It should also include their percentage of ownership and relationship to the others (maybe they have worked together in the past). If there will be changes in ownership under this plan, it should be explained as well. There should also be a summary of major stockholders, boards of directors, or other ownership charts provided.

Management Team. Brief description of Senior Management. This is one of the most important paragraphs in the plan. Resumes shall be provided in the supporting documents but a brief summary shall be presented here. The SBA and the bankers that are SBA lenders are currently seeking clients with five years minimum experience in their chosen business sector.

Staffing. This should provide the number of employees and divisions. Company's staffing and labor as it is now and as in the future. An organizational chart is helpful in this section. It should include: Type of labor (skilled, unskilled and professional); Where are the employees going to be recruited from; Pay structure; Training; Job descriptions; Independent contractors; Outsourcing.

The production process. How is the product or service produced and/or distributed? Explain the methods of: Production techniques; Quality control; Customer service.

Supply Chain Management. What levels of supply chain management are keys to the business? A vertically integrated business has multiple aspects of the supply chain. These are the eleven major supply chains: Raw material acquisition; Product Development, Design, Multiphase pre-fabrication, etc.; Manufacturing; Packaging for authorized distributors and brokers; Tracking systems (RFID tags or other technology solutions implemented); Shipping; Brokerage/Jobber; Warehousing; Shipping to Wholesalers; Retail Broker; Retail Sales. Other supply chain issues to discuss include: Names and addresses of suppliers; Type and amount of inventory furnished; Credit and delivery policies; History and reliability; Back-Up suppliers.

Location/Facilities. The location choice should be made with the help of a qualified commercial real estate agent. A professional in the industry can assist in creating the best location for the business and its customers. Key issues to consider include: Square Footage and other location needs; Type of building; Zoning (commercial, industrial, manufacturing, retail, office, etc.); Power and other utilities access issues – is the correct power structure available to support the business; Parking and accessibility to the freeway, airports, railroads or shipping centers; Consider including a drawing or layout of the proposed facility; If new construction is planned, then a summary of it should be provided here and drawings shall be in the supporting documents; Is a conditional use permit (CUP) needed?; Will engineering, planning, and safety in city hall approve the business?

Hours of operation. What is the justification? Who is being served by being open these hours?

Legal Issues. Include the following (and always consult an attorney is this area). Business Entity (discussed in section two about the company but here why the entity was chosen should be explained). Licensing/bonding. Is this a professional corporation with attorneys, accountants, real estate agents, insurance agents or other licensed professionals? Business licensing should also be mentioned for both city, county, state or federal requirements; Permits; Environmental regulations; Zoning or building codes; Insurance coverage; Trademarks, copyrights, and/or patents (pending, existing or purchased).

Inventory. If the business has inventory, then an inventory plan is a crucial aspect of the business. How will it be paid for (accounts receivable loans or other methods)? How much inventory must be on hand and why? What will be the ongoing wholesale and retail value of the inventory? How often will it turnover. What is the lad time from ordering to deliver? Is it coming from out of the country? Is it raw materials or finished product?

Professional/Advisory Team. Provide a list of names, addresses, telephone numbers and email addresses of the advisory team. Ensure that the advisers know they are in the plan and may be called by financiers or other persons reading the plan. The list should include, at a minimum, the following professionals: Professional employer or Payroll Company, Business Plan writer, Web Developer, Attorney, Accountant, Banker, Consultant and/or financial planners, Insurance broker, Real Estate Broker, Computer, IT, or MIS consultants.

Section 7 - Exit Strategy. The exit strategy is critical. The entire plan should begin with the end in mind – what is the company trying to accomplish in the long run? What will happen when the major milestones are achieved? How will the management team continue on with the company as it grows? Will the company sell, be acquired, acquire other companies, prepare an initial public offering? Is there is a stock buyout or buy-back plan? What happens if the principals become incapacitated by divorce, injury, or even death?

Exits strategies are all about planning for the future of the business. As uncomfortable as it is to think about it, a business owner isn't going to be around forever. What will happen to the business in the event of his death, or if he becomes incapacitated, or if he just decides it's time to retire? Who will own the company? Who will run the company?

Exit strategies answer those questions as well as a slew of others:

- If the company is owned in a partnership:
    - Is there key man insurance to cover the cost of replacing a partner (management wise) in the event of his death or incapacitation?
    - If one of the partners decides he wants to sell his share of the company, do the remaining partners have the right of first refusal regarding the purchase of those shares? Is there an agreement in place that the remaining partners have some say in who purchases those shares?
    - If one of the partners dies and his surviving family members assume ownership of his share of the company, and they decide to sell,

do the remaining partners have the right of first refusal for the purchase of those shares?

- If one of the partners dies and a surviving member of his family assumes ownership of his share in the company, and that member is unqualified to assume a management position but wants to, is there a plan in place to prevent that from happening?
- At what level of company revenue would the owner consider hiring a senior management team and assume a position on the board of directors?
- At what level of company revenue and/or value would the owner consider selling the company?
- Is there a time-line established when a venture capitalist investor in the company will be able to cash out his investment or be bought out?
- At what point would the company consider an initial public offering (IPO) for the company? How will that affect ownership and management?

There are other things to consider, but these provide some examples. The point is that business owners need to plan for the long-term future of the company.

Section 8 - General Supporting documents. Supporting documents are the foundation of a business plan. Without them, there is little validity in the plan. The supporting documents should provide summaries of the material provided in the plan. However, the total sum of the supporting documents should not overburden the reader. In some instances it may make sense to have the supporting documents accumulated in a separate booklet. Within the actual business plan, the supporting documents should not exceed 10 to 20 pages. At a minimum they should include:

1. Brochures and advertising materials;
2. Industry studies;

3. Blueprints and plans;
4. Maps and photos of location;
5. Magazine or other articles;
6. Detailed lists of equipment owned or to be purchased;
7. Copies of leases and contracts;
8. Letters of support from future customers;
9. Any other materials needed to support the assumptions in this plan;
10. Market research studies;
11. List of assets available as collateral for a loan.

Industry Trends Research. Substantial documentation verifying claims should be included in the supporting documents as well. This may be reports from third party companies or universities. They may be quotes from industry data reports. They may be newspaper articles that provide secondary research. They may be reports provided by association memberships. As it is with the supporting documents, the industry trend research should not exceed ten pages.

Section 9 – References & Citations. For many business plans, this is the most important section. The references and citations should VALIDATE the claims being made. Primary and secondary research sources should be located here as well as interviews, potential client preliminary talks, third party validation firms, testing laboratories results, etc. Proving the potential success of a business model is the primary purpose of a business plan. Provide the support material bibliography here to substantiate the claims being made.

Our next "Heros" are the founders of DJ Safety, Retired Navy Commander Joseph Hansen and his wife Darlene (Deist) Hansen. Since 1996 they have built a high-level design engineering company for specific industries and the U.S. Government.

There custom safety assembly system have been built for the aerospace, aviation, film and theme ride industries as well as racing safety assemblies. Some of the key projects they have completed include the development and fabrication of ballistic containment for presses at the LA Times, design development of auxiliary turbine containment devices for NASA, F-16X lead wing project and many other projects for private and public companies.

What made the Hansen's become one of our hero's is their amazing ability to keep going when times are tough. The racing, aerospace, and Hollywood budgets have all dropped considerable over the past few years but Joe kept going,. He has kept his staff employed working on a maraud of projects not part of their core business in odder to stay afloat. They pursued and were approved for creative financing methods in order to keep cash flowing at a time when most might have given up. They are true Americans and serve our county with a level of loyalty, patriotism and commitment that is beyond the call of duty – we are proud to call them friends and clients.

154

CHAPTER 4
MARKETING

We would like to thank Robert Fukui and Jeff Ray of *High Point Marketing, Inc.*; J Michael Palka of *Winning Spirit Marketing*; and Adam Blejski of *Parallel6* for their contributions in compiling this section of *The Business Owner's Handbook*.

Introduction to marketing. Outside of cash flow and reserve shortages, the second highest reason for business failure is the lack of a well budgeted and executed marketing plan. This chapter will describe all facets of a solid plan and defines a plethora of terms used. We'll start with marketing itself - SUMATICI has developed the following definition: *"Marketing is a business concept in which an organization creates a process of informing, arousing and ultimately acquiring and maintaining customer relationships. A properly managed marketing plan links a company to the customer by engaging the buyer in ways that they may not have otherwise purchased without the marketing effort. The process of marketing is multifaceted as it is a coordinated effort of operations being in balance with marketing, advertising, sales, media, public relations, branding and the Internet - all designed in an effort to gain and keep customers for long term growth."*

Philosophy. The first thing on our clients mind when we initially meet is "what's the best way to advertise for increased sales?" Unfortunately most clients focus on sales – but that is only the end result. The small businesses we consult mix their idea of marketing with advertising and sales. While commercials, print ads, jazzy websites, and billboards are some examples of promotional vehicles that can get the word out about a product or service, they are only one aspect of marketing. Our philosophy is that the most overlooked aspect of marketing for small business is that advertising, sales, customer service and retention programs are the combined effort called *marketing*. It is one thing to gain customers, it is another to retain them and make them repeat ones. It is far less expensive to maintain an existing customer than to gain a new one. What most organizations don't understand is that if they don't treat their customer's right and keep in contact, they may be out of sight and out of mind. If a company attracts 11 customers but loses 10, the net gain is only one new customer.

Marketing and selling. The basic difference between marketing and selling is that marketing identifies a business while selling is the relationship created between the business and its customers. Selling can be the most challenging aspect of running a business. As the life cycle of a product or service changes, so might the sales cycle. Here is an example of a typical sales cycle:

Step 1 – Gather the prospects. The target audience is important. The highest return on time and money comes from being in the right market. Don't waste time and money unless the buyer being presented to fits the target market. Our goal is *rifle targeting* instead of *shotgun targeting*. Know exactly who the customer is. Research them. If it is a business, know the business before approaching them. Purchase accurate lists.

Step 2 - Gather information. Gather information about the target market before and during your contact with them. Learn about their business so the presentation makes it obvious they need the product or service. Take away objections with knowledge. Marketing is gaining – and keeping – customers. All the ways to communicate with potential customers – needs to have a consistent message about your business: what do you want them to know about you?

Step 3 – *Present the product or service*. Focus on how purchasing the product or service benefits them. Do not focus on the features. Remember that a feature is a fact. No one wants to hear facts. Unfortunately, most salespeople focus on the facts. However, a benefit is how the product or service makes them *feel*. Make sure that when presenting, have the buyer feel positive about the benefits and the process become much easier.

Step 4 – *Let the potential buyer try the product or service without obligation*. Now that the need has been established, have them try it. Would you buy a pair of shoes without trying them on? or buy a car with a test drive? or perfume without smelling it? If testing is not an option, then provide references.

Step 5 – *Ask them to purchase*. By following steps one through four, step five is easy. Step one established them as a viable client whom could benefit; step two researched their firm to ensure the presentation was accurate; step three listened to the client and found out they need the product; and step four presented the product and let them try it. So ask them to buy! Step five is the one step skipped most often. "Are you prepared to purchase the product today?"

Step 6 – *Show appreciation*. Thank them for purchasing and follow-up for customer service. Send them a thank you card! Follow up with a survey.

Step 7 – *Follow up a second time*. One month later, when the customer is satisfied with your product/service(s), ask for referrals.

Target market. These are the people who will buy the product or service. Learn their location (geographically), their number (demographics, including age, sex and disposable income), and how many of them in that total potential customer pool are buying what the products/services offered. What do they know about the business and the products/services being offered? If the company has been in business for awhile, ask the clients to fill out a survey at the check-out counter. (To motivate them, offer them a small discount on their next purchase.) Find out what they think and what they would like to see regarding the business. Even if the company is a start-up, seek to find out from trade association publications, Internet research, or just visiting with customers in a competitor's store why they buy the product or service.

What does the company want the customer to know about the business? Now make a list of everything the customers ought to know that will encourage them to buy. Then pare it down to one sentence of 25 words or less. Why? Because a marketing message which is reproduced in all company communications with potential customers can only say so much. So what are the things a customer absolutely needs to know in order to buy from the company? Now ask, "Why should they believe you?" People are literally bombarded everyday with advertising that promises everything from the freshest breath to hot dates. And because people hear advertising claims all the time, they are skeptical and cynical. The answer can't be a detailed list of features (the competition's "stuff" probably has the same or very similar features). The answer has to be focused on the unique benefits the company's product or service offers that customer that they can count on.

Communicate the message. What information must be included in the marketing? Well let's start with contact information: Include the business location address, phone number(s) and website address. Also, include the company logo and tag line. Add any legal or copyright lines that may be necessary. And finally, specific photos should also be included.

How will the company evaluate the effectiveness of its marketing? First, when employees have direct contact with customers, have the employees ask them how they heard about the business. (This includes phone conversations and check-out counter experiences.) Was it through word-of-mouth? An advertisement? The Yellow Pages? What? And track it with a simple checklist by the phone or at the cash register. Also, if the company offers coupons or discounts in the advertisements, track their redemption rate. Second, find out how many people are visiting the business website, how long they stay, and what site pages they're looking at while there. Most of the time, the people who maintain the website can provide that information.

How much can the company budget afford? This is last because thinking about all the options to determine which ones will work best for the company as well as which ones the company can afford is necessary. A budget will cause a business to evaluate what marketing strategy will provide the most "bang for the buck." At the same time, having a budget may force the management to plan on marketing in phases, building on each step to create an entire message about the business. Remember, the marketing plan and budget is a forecast so must make sense.

Situation Analysis. What niche is being filled with the product or service, what market will pay for it? Answer the "who, what, when, where, how and why" of the marketing plan. What is the stage of development of the company and product or service and is the operational team prepared to support the marketing team – and vice versa.

Marketing Strategy. Overview of the company's marketing, advertising, promotions, methods of distribution and/or sales force. The Marketing Strategy should identify:
1. Geography,
2. Mass marketing;
3. Direct marketing; and
4. Local opportunities.

Primary Target Market. Who are the customers? (Who spends money for this product/service?) Is it a business-to-consumer business or business-to-business or business to government? Where does the company fall in the supply chain? Is it a distributor, wholesaler or retailer? Does it sell to the end consumer and/or the middleman?

Demographics B2C, B2B, B2G. Create a demographic profile of the intended target audience. The profile should include:
1. Age;
2. Gender;
3. Location;
4. Income level;
5. Social class and occupation;
6. Education.

The more unique the product/service the larger the radius of the market. The majority of companies are small businesses and are located in a certain area. Research the average or median income, the number of people, and their race and ethnicities in that market area. These factors will affect the company's marketing. When making claims about the size of a target market, the company should have three references like the U.S. Census, city government, and cities.com. (See

160

below for a listing of sources for demographic information.) If three different numbers are presented form these sources then use "an estimate". Don't say things like "about"; show exact amounts from the research.

Sources of Information. The U.S. Census Bureau – American Fact Finder – is always the best place to start (http://factfinder.census.gov/home/saff/aff_transition.html). Searches can be done by zip code, city or county. As of this writing many searches include the 2000 census info, and the site is quickly updating with the new 2010 census info. Another advantage to this site is the American Community Survey (ACS) info from 2005-2006. If some searches of the census data aren't up to date, the ACS search can be helpful.

Citydata.com is another useful tool. To search, just type in a city name. Usually most current information is available. However, the site doesn't always have every area. Searches can also be done on city web sites which have demographic information. But be cautious: some sites are not always accurate. (Always look for a second source to confirm the results.) Searches by specific counties can also be done for some demographic information.

Primary Market Research. This is research conducted by the company about the market and potential customers within the market. Primary research means the company gathers its own data. Professional market research can be very costly; but there are many books that show small business owners how to do effective research themselves. When writing the marketing plan, be as specific as possible: give statistics, numbers and sources.

Stakeholders, Strategic Alliances, and Collaborators. These include small businesses that service the same market; large businesses that service the same target audience;

associations; memberships, or clubs. For small businesses (under $5 million) strategic alliances, partnerships, collaborators are very important. These business relationships can produce revenue for the company, both directly and indirectly. Networking and building strategic alliances in which the business can partner with other business owners and promote each other is another cost effective element of marketing. Even *Fortune 500* companies utilize this strategy to increase their sales and marketing efforts. *McDonald's* and *Disney* have established a long term alliance for many years. Every time *Disney* releases a new animated film, they partner with *McDonald's* to promote the film by offering action figures from the film to be part of the "Happy Meal." This alliance makes sense because both *McDonald's* and *Disney* are targeting the same audience: children. *McDonald's* with their "Happy Meals" and *Disney* with their action figures jointly raise the level of awareness of their brand and ultimately sell more than if they tried to do it alone.

Stakeholders. Businesses or organizations that have a stake in the deal but no consideration (monetary benefit). There is some kind of contract, a fee, or rules which have to be followed. These would include memberships or associations like the chamber of commerce or a trade/industry association.

Alliance. When both parties have an agreement in writing in which one or both sides benefit by making money from the alliance. Examples would be: Financial adviser - by referring a client the company doesn't get paid (a financial adviser is required to have a NASD license to have commission), but the referral is a benefit to a client. Strategic alliance with a payroll company – for every client the company refers to them, the company gets a percentage of their payroll fees.

Collaborators. No contract exists, however working together helps both organizations succeed. For example, a business plan development company collaborates with a bank regarding business loans. Neither side gets paid directly for the collaboration, but without the collaboration both sides lose business opportunities. So both sides refer clients to each other.

Secondary Market Research. Secondary research means using published information such as industry profiles, trade journals, newspapers, magazines, census data and demographic profiles. This type of information is available in public libraries, industry associations, chambers of commerce, from vendors who sell to the industry and from government agencies. This section should not be a list of all the secondary research but an explanation of what was found out from the research. Secondary market research supports other parts of the marketing plan. What supports company strategy in the beginning of the entire plan? What supports situation analysis? Always cross reference the secondary information because one source can't reliably determine if statements or claims are correct. Usually a good place to start is with government resources at local, state and federal level. The government (at all levels) spends billions of dollars annually to create this information and provide it to the public for free and online. Also use media sources such as periodicals, journals, newspapers, etc. Industries also provide this information through trade associations or industry groups. Internet searches can be helpful and access many of these resources quickly. One word of caution: *Wikipedia* not a good secondary research source, but can be a useful guide to get research started. The articles have resources at the bottom (references and citations) which can be used to do some secondary research.

Competitive Analysis. A competitive analysis will provide an overview of the competition from the standpoint of the total competitive outlook. The analysis should review the total market potential, how the company's differentiation provides a competitive advantage over both direct and indirect competition based on a number of factors including features, benefits, and price. How are other companies presenting their products? This should only be an overview as the details of competition are further discussed in the plan. This section may not be written first, because it is actually an overview of the next few sections. However, it is important: many investors will read it. The next five or six paragraphs need to support what is written here. It doesn't have to be too long - maybe a couple of paragraphs - but it should explain what makes one business better than another.

Direct Competition. These are companies chasing after the exact same client with their marketing dollars. And these companies are essentially the same: size, market share, customer, product or service. The difference comes down to who has the better product, service, and/or price, and marketing plan.

Major Competitors (Comparison Chart). Complete a competitive analysis (include a chart) directly comparing the competing companies. The chart should include key products, locations, customers, price, and key differentiation issues. There is no standardized chart, but whatever chart is designed, it should be easy to read and reader friendly. Look for what makes sense. The chart should put the top six to ten companies compared to the company the marketing plan is written for. Generally speaking compare similar sized companies, unless, of course there is a two year old company with a clear advantage over a billion dollar company.

The chart should be "slanted" to help present the company in a favorable light, and to highlight the company's benefits and features. After all, the ultimate goal is to get the funding being sought. However, that's not a license to lie or present misinformation. First, that would be unethical, and second, it will be found out and company credibility will be lost (along with the opportunity to get the funding needed). The point is if it is too difficult to present the business' competitive advantage through a chart, the company may have difficulty being successful.

Several different comparisons can be used to reflect one of the company's competitive advantages: price, safety, speed, guarantees, effectiveness, etc. Sometimes a comparison chart may include a comparison of several features or benefits – if that best reflects the company. Other times a chart may only compare a specific feature or benefit that shows the product or service is the better one.

It is important to list the competitors. For small businesses working within a particular geographic area a search of online yellow pages can be done and competitors can be cut and pasted into a list. This list also provides an address or phone number in order to find out: 1) How much the competitors are charging for the same product? (A visit to the store may be necessary to find out.) And 2) if competitors charge less than the business does (or the general market) how are they doing that? (This may sometimes involve proprietary information and therefore be more difficult to obtain. But, again, visit the store and ask and see what happens.)

Indirect Competitive Factors. Indirect competitive factors are companies, products, services, or even individual efforts to accomplish, in another way, the very thing the business' products or services offer to accomplish. For example, a retail coffee business that sells cups of coffee may also sell bagged coffee by the pound. Direct competitors may be other coffee shops while indirect competitors may be grocery stores or specialty coffee stores that sell coffee by the pound. Think from the client's perspective: if a customer has limited resources, where else could he go to spend his money?

Sustainable Competitive Advantage. As the market and economic changes occur, is there a competitive advantage the company will always have over its competitors, which will help it to continue to succeed? For instance, if the company has a new technology that beats the competition, how will it stay ahead of them after the technology becomes commonplace? Maybe the business has other research and development plans for furthering its technology or other products, or maybe the company's target market is different and its competition will not access them for some reason that can be explained. This can include patents, trademarks, copyrights, or a new twist on an old idea.

Market Size, Market Share, Market Penetration. What is the total size of the business' market in the geographical area it will compete in? The objective in market share analysis is to demonstrate the market is large enough to support substantial sales growth or to demonstrate the market is not currently being satisfactorily served by competitors. Then develop an argument through research that the company can penetrate a certain percentage of the market over time through an aggressive marketing campaign. A simple example would be a market in which there are 99 competitors that have varying degrees of market share. But the top three have 90% of the market and the start-up intends to be number four with a 3% share. How will the company attain this goal?

Barriers to Entry. How difficult will it be for competitors to copy the business' model? This should be more than money related. If all it takes is for a wealthy person to fund a competitor, the business does not have a viable sustainable advantage nor does it have viable barriers to entry. Here are some of the key aspects to barriers to entry that can help in combating competitors:

1. High capital costs;
2. High production costs;
3. High marketing costs;
4. Consumer acceptance;
5. Brand recognition;
6. Uniquely trained staff, exceptional training and skills;
7. Unique technology and patents;
8. Trademarks;
9. Unions;
10. Shipping costs;
11. Tariff barriers and quotas;
12. Change in technology;
13. Change in government regulations;
14. Change in the economy;
15. Change in your industry.

SWOT Analysis. Every person who evaluates businesses looks for a SWOT analysis. SWOT analysis is a common business practice even though it involves a lot of intuition and subjectivity. Here are some guidelines:

1. The SWOT analysis is easier to write if the Weaknesses and Threats first are examined first. Once those are identified, counterbalance them with the Strengths and Opportunities.

2. When presenting Weaknesses and Threats, don't say things like, "Our management team is weak" or "China is investing large capital outlays to increase market share and drive small businesses out of the

market." Instead, present a solution that lets the investor or lender know the company is aware of its weaknesses or threats and is acting to solve them: "The company ownership and current management are seeking to hire experienced and successful managerial staff" or "Due to China's efforts to increase market share, our company will engage in an aggressive local marketing campaign emphasizing our competitive prices and our 'Made in the U.S.A.' label." As much as possible, have all four sections take up one full page. Because investors and lenders read the SWOT analysis, make it as easy as possible.

Strengths (Internal) - What are the overall strengths of the business (product, price, staff, and advantages)?

Weaknesses (Internal) - Where is the company or product weak and vulnerable (opposite of strengths in staff, product, price, etc.).

Opportunities (External) - What factors in the macro economic outlook provide opportunities for the company?

Threats (External) - What global influences cause risk to the business (global economics, currency rates, weather, etc.).

Product Distribution Channels. How does the business sell its products or services? (This depends on where it is in the supply chain.) Channels include:
1. Retail;
2. Direct (mail order, Web, catalog);
3. Wholesale;
4. Your own sales force;
5. Agents;
6. Independent representatives;
7. Bid on contracts.

Placement. Analyze the company's location criteria as they will affect your customers. Is the location of the business important to its customers? If yes, how? If customers come to the place of business:
1. Is it convenient?
2. Is there parking?
3. Is there enough interior space?
4. Is it consistent with the company's image?
5. Is it what customers want and expect?
6. Where is the competition located?
7. Is it better to be near the competition?
8. How will you get the product to market?
9. What channels of distribution will be used?
10. Will the company sell directly to the end user or wholesale the product?

Promotion. Outside sales representatives (Commissioned or non-commissioned); In-house sales force. (Commissioned or non commissioned); Will the company license the product and have someone else market the product? How will the business tell its customers the product is available? Through word of mouth; referrals; advertising through print, TV, newspaper, radio, direct mail, websites, brochures, coupon or co-op?

Guerrilla marketing is one form of marketing for small business owners. The objective of guerrilla marketing is to create a unique, engaging and thought-provoking concept to generate buzz, and consequently turn viral. The term was coined and defined by Jay Conrad Levinson in his book *Guerrilla Marketing*. The term has since entered the popular vocabulary and marketing textbooks.

Price. Explain the method(s) of setting prices (is it consumer driven, competition driven, supply/demand issues, etc.?).

Does the pricing strategy fit with what was revealed in the competitive analysis? (The old fashioned way: Cost + Profit = Sales Price.) A price comparison chart is an effective tool in this section.

Competitive pricing: Price based on 'what the traffic will bear' and the competitive forces. (Be careful that 'price' always exceeds 'cost.') Industrial/commercial products and many services 'price' is only one factor in the customer's decision process, but remember 'price is always an issue'.

What will be company customer service and credit policies? *Website and social media.* If the business already has a website, this section should give an overview of the purpose of the website. Web page examples should be placed in the supporting documents if they have already been created. Put the domain name here and then fill out this section by outlining the home page tabs. Follow that information by explaining the following:
1. Is the website designed for information or e-commerce or both?
2. How is the system integrated into the overall sales plan?
3. How does the website get marketed online?
4. Are there outside marketing and advertising plans designed to drive people to the website?
5. What programming issues are important?
6. Is there a back office system, a database, or online training?
7. How is search engine optimization and social media integrated into the web presence?

Social Media – More than Virtual Word of Mouth. Companies across the globe, whether they are *Fortune 500* or start-ups, wrestle with the concept of social media solutions for business and how to best utilize them. Many question the degree to which social media can provide value to their

170

business model and produce results. The concern is valid. Any time, money or effort utilized by an organization to pursue something fairly new should be scrutinized and thoroughly researched. It should be determined that the activity supports a goal or multiple goals of the organization. For most, social media will most likely be one activity among many that supports specific goals and functions within a business.

A growing number of marketers believe it is safe to say that social media is here to stay in the short to medium term and deserves to be considered by business owners and managers worldwide.

Before addressing the role social media can play in business, it's important to reflect on the current trends of consumers and businesses involved in social media. 67% of consumer purchase decisions are primarily influenced by Word of Mouth (*The Consumer Decision Journey*, 2009, McKinsey), which social media supports as its core function. Nearly a quarter of social network users indicated that Facebook is the number one social site or service that influences their buying decisions. [Source: Tom Webster, *the Social Habit*]. EMarketer predicts that spending on social media will be up 55% from 2010 for US marketers and will rise by a further 27.7% in 2012. Facebook has almost 700 million users worldwide (almost 150 million in the US alone) and all other social properties are still growing at high rates such as *LinkedIn* with 33.4 million visitors, 58% growth in the past year, and *Tumblr* with 10.7 million visitors, 166% growth in the past year. Social media can be very powerful when it is combined with other marketing activities to affect the areas of branding, marketing, R&D, customer service and advertising for a company.

EBranding. Consumers are logging into social media en masse. They spend time conversing, researching and more in social media. With the amount of time consumers spend within social media channels, it is essential for a company to be present in the channels and for the channels to portray the company as it would in print, radio, TV and web. A company's brand should be recognizable in social media just like any other avenue of brand recognition. Logo, color palettes, typeface, taglines, imagery, company voice and more should be established throughout social media assets (such as Facebook) to reflect a consistent brand across all efforts (online and offline).

EMarketing. There are several tools companies use to constantly connect with new consumers and keep their present or past customers in their orbit and engaged (staying top of mind). Email marketing, mailers, client events and more have been utilized over the years to varying degrees of effectiveness depending on the company. Social media is another tool in the business tool belt to be leveraged. Social media is a useful system for creating a virtual and interactive "client for life" program. Utilized correctly, social media can connect NEW micro-targeted and qualified consumers; connect with existing or past clients; open two-way communications with new, present and past customers; keep them constantly engaged with useful information, tips, conversations and more; and act as a barometer for consumer feelings about services and product offerings.

By utilizing techniques unique to each social media channel, companies can grow a fan base that is engaged and actionable over time, not just in the short term. For example, a company could employ a Facebook ads strategy or contest strategy aimed at attracting a very specific demographic within the Facebook user base. Is the "perfect" potential client 34-45 year of age, female, lives within 50 miles of downtown Chicago, likes Chanel and has at least one child of the age 0-3 years? She can be identified along with all others who qualify in the group, advertised to directly within her Facebook session and be made a connection (of her own will by clicking a company's ad) within Facebook utilizing Facebook ads. Once she has been made a fan of the company, it is the responsibility of the company's Community Manager to keep her engaged with great content (blogs, posts, videos, info, and tips) and offer contests that keep things fun and interesting. Done correctly, the company could keep this micro-targeted user in their orbit and keep the brand top of mind for months and years.

EAdvertising. Once captured, the user base within social media can be leveraged for profit. The typical modis operandi for companies who utilize social media effectively is to insert calls-to-action (offers, discounts, buy now, etc.) throughout their typical messaging and interaction with social media followers. However, more aggressive approaches to posting offers and "buy now" type messaging can work for some companies. For example, if a company is a discount jeweler and most fans are there to get the latest and greatest deals on the cheap, it might make sense to post "buy now" calls-to-action more frequently than say BMW. Regardless of determined frequency of offers, it's clear a micro-targeted social media following is a great place to insert advertising messaging for the sake of revenue.

R&D – Social Media allows real-time feedback from the key demographic buyer pool the company has attracted. New service, service offerings, product changes and branding initiatives can all be tested via social media at a fraction of the cost of traditional R&D.

Customer Service. Allowing a constantly monitored forum and community for consumers to interact provides the perfect place to involve customer service initiatives. Consumers constantly comment, "like" and share posts within social media, many of which require a response from the company. Social media creates a system that provides a one-to-one and public real-time forum to address concerns, answer questions, resolve problems and spread service and product news to those interested.

In summary, social media can be a wonderful medium to leverage for your branding, marketing and advertising efforts along with R&D and customer service. Keep in mind, attention still must always be paid to traditional efforts (outbound sales, print advertising, trade shows, etc.) with social media amplifying or supporting those efforts.

Mobile Marketing. An area close to social media that may be worth as much or more attention currently is mobile marketing, which will become invaluable in the near future as consumers migrate to handheld devices over the use of computers and laptops. One of the most significant changes impacting consumers over the past few years is the proliferation of Smart Phones and Tablet computers. The number of Smartphone users worldwide is predicted to exceed one billion by 2014 (Parks Associates, 2010) and *Forrester Research* delivered a new forecast in January of 2011 expecting the number of tablets sold in the U.S. to go from 10.3 million in 2010 to 24.1 million in 2011, and growing to 44 million in annual units sold by 2015. At that point, by 2015, it projects that 82 million people in the U.S. will own some sort of tablet, or a full one third of the online population.

Smartphone's and tablets have rapidly become our most intimate piece of technology, either attached to us, or nearby, for more than 16 hours per day. For the first time, in June of 2011, time spent with mobile apps per day per person reached an average of 81 minutes compared to 74 minutes on the Web, according to advertising firm *Flurry*. With that companies at all stages of development are looking for ways to build their brands and drive revenue through this channel.

As this mobile channel has grown, so has the complexity of Mobile Marketing. Today's Mobile Marketing ecosystem includes Mobile Apps, Mobile Websites, SMS Campaigns, Location Based Services and Geo Targeting, Bluetooth and WiFi Advertising, Pay Per Click and Paid Media, M-commerce and M Wallet initiatives, AdverGames and so on. New game changing technologies, such as Augmented Reality, will continue to impact this space for years to come.

How do you navigate through this constantly evolving world of Mobile Marketing? Start by answering the following key strategy questions:

1. What business goals are we trying to achieve?
2. What products and services will we promote through the Mobile channel?
3. Who is our customer and what is the best vehicle to reach them? For example, if you're targeting a certain demographic, are they *iPhone*, *iPad*, *Android* or *Blackberry* users? Or, does your demographic not have a Smartphone and might SMS be the better choice?
4. Should we create your own Mobile App? What user experience will we deliver through our App? Users will quickly delete Apps that do not provide value on a frequent basis. What's our strategy to market the app and gain adoption?
5. What content and messaging will we use and in what format; written, video or audio?
6. What promotions and/or offers will we provide?

What are the best vehicles for advertising these offers; ads on games, pay per click, banners on mobile sites, SMS opt in campaigns, ads on WiFi servers? Can we leverage other providers such as daily deal companies, coupon aggregators, etc. who already have a mobile presence?

1. What is our expected return on investment from mobile and how will we measure this? What metrics will we use, how will we track and how often will we report?
2. How flexible is our strategy? If the numbers aren't trending, how easy will it be to change course?
3. How will we integrate our mobile strategy with our social media or other online marketing initiatives? Are there opportunities for better outcomes through and integrated strategy?

Finally, if you're having trouble determining your Mobile strategy, or need help with execution, hire a Mobile Marketing agency. They'll guide you through the process, select the appropriate technologies, design and execute campaigns and measure success.

Advertising Budget. What is the market driver(s) that cause people to purchase this product or service? How much will it cost to market the product? How much money does it take to get the product into people's hands? What is the sales commission that will have to be paid? How much will it cost to keep customers (Customer Retention Management (CRM))? When writing this section, talk about specific ways and means of spending the money. Also discuss alliances and partnerships that may be formed or that may already be present. Many are not free and may be very expensive: contract fees, services, commissions, pay-per-client, etc. This is another section in which a chart or spreadsheet should be utilized. It should include a three to four year plan with the years across the top and the budget line items on the left with the actual dollar figures in the cells. The line items should include:

1. Website expenses;
2. Media;
3. Newspapers;
4. Magazines;
5. Radio;
6. TV (Cable);
7. Direct Mail;
8. Talk Fusion (email videos);
9. Promotions;
10. Brochures;
11. Coupons;
12. Newsletters; and
13. Trade shows.

While salaries for the sales team is usually included under payroll expenses, don't forget that a sales commission is a cost of getting the product or service into a consumer's hands.

Branding/Graphic Imagery. Remember to present a single and consistent message about the company in all advertising and branding. That "message" should be present in all the ways the company interacts with the public, and especially its target market. Branding and graphic design should include strategies of:
1. Color;
2. Logo design – the company name should always be included in the logo whenever possible;
3. Cards and letterhead;
4. Brochures;
5. Signage; and
6. Interior design.

If the company has a slogan, include it here. And place graphic examples of the logo and other graphics here as well.

Customer Retention Management (CRM). The business must have a plan to retain existing customers. A system should be developed that identifies existing customers and then systematically contacts them for repeat business. Businesses that do not harness this skill realize one of the greatest failures of business – what is being done to keep them coming back and referring their friends and associates? When a client knows a company really cares, he will be a client for life. Generally, it's a good idea to use the following formula to budget for your CRM: 40% budget should be straight call to action advertising; 40% branding; 20% customer retention. Over time, hitting benchmarks and milestones would change the percent of the budget for each of these items. Touch customers six times per year to maintain communication and remain in their minds. One simple way of doing this is SendOutCards.com. This online service allows a business to maintain a customer database and either manually send a real greeting card or schedule the system to send a card on a regular basis.

Sales Cycle. Business owners often fail to recognize the value in creating a comprehensive sales cycle. Every business has one. The first step in the cycle is customer contact (how did it occur?). The last step is transacting business, meaning the customer pays for the product or service. The cycle includes everything in between those two steps. So ask: How does the company get customers to investigate its products/services? How does it get them to purchase? What is the cycle that the business must create and maintain for constant customer flow? Things to consider include the following example:
1. Retrieve Calls or intercepting customers at the door;
2. Ask the customer what their needs are to determine the best way to suit their needs;
3. Show the customer how their needs may be met by the company;

4. Ask them to purchase;
5. Collect payment;
6. Deliver the product and/or service;
7. Follow-up for customer satisfaction;
8. Implement the customer retention management system as discussed previously.

Grass-Roots Campaign. A grass-roots campaign gets the company's customer base excited. The word-of-mouth method of advertising is known as "grass-roots." How will the business get the word out to customers? A grass-roots campaign with 1,000 satisfied customers is quite powerful – but how does the business get the first 1,000? Can the media be helpful? Does the company have a special promotion that will get free advertising? Identify low-cost methods to get the most out of the promotional budget. Use methods other than paid advertising, such as trade shows, catalogs, dealer incentives, word of mouth and network of friends or professionals.

Public Relations. Many entrepreneurs overlook the power of Public Relations -- and that's a big mistake. PR can create exposure more effectively than hard-dollar advertising, and cost considerably less. A properly structured PR campaign can influence the target market in a way that advertising alone cannot.

Public Relations are another way to market and brand a company through two strategies: First, keeping the public informed about the business through regular press releases and/media events about events, changes or new product/service introduction involving the company. Second, involve the business actively and visibly in the support of a non-profit or charitable cause or organization. Public relations includes:
1. Press release calendar;

2. Press kit;
3. Media events.

PR does more than promote a product or service; it promotes goodwill between the company and the public. As a practice of communications management between an organization and the public, PR generates exposure using topics of public interest to create news items and third-party endorsements without any sales pitch. It encourages a third party -- such as a newspaper, conference organizer, etc. -- to give its stamp of credibility to the company without a sales pitch that requires consumers to simply take the company's word for it. But it also casts a wide net with the right strategy: anything from speaking engagements to crisis communication and even social media and employee communication. So, take a look at three of the most important facets of PR program development:

The Press Kit. The Press Kit remains the most important tool in any PR campaign. It provides the media with materials for developing a story about the company and its management, whether as a physical printed portfolio, digital media which is distributed directly (CDs, DVDs, flash drives, etc.) or even an entire online digital media room. What goes into a good Press Kit?
1. Biographies
2. Press Releases
3. Photos
4. Videos (online)
5. Fact Sheet
6. Articles
7. Media Clips (of previous media reviews)
8. Audios.

The Press Release. If a Press Kit is a hammer, the Press Release is a jack hammer. The most import thing to keep in mind about a release, however, remains that it's NOT a sales piece. It is used to communicate a newsworthy story directly to the media and, ultimately, to the target market. Writing a proper Press Release that the media will take the time to review and consider comes with practice and study. Don't be misled to think that press releases are easy to do. Hire a professional, and the investment will prove it worthwhile many times over.

Crisis Plan. Most entrepreneurs overlook that something may unexpectedly damage their credibility, costing their sales and even possibly the entire business. Cultivating continued media relations and coverage represents the beginning of a Crisis Plan. Nurturing those relationships offers the company an opportunity to tell the business' side of a story without bias. Maintaining a publicist or company spokesperson who deals with the media remains essential for a crisis plan; and the company should periodically develop and review a checklist of things that might go wrong, and strategies for how to best respond.

Of course, Public Relations involve much more than these few items. Check out a few of the many books on the subject, but don't expect to become an expert in a day, a week or even a year. The best way to learn about PR is to start and remain consistent. Put time into PR efforts every month. The more effort made, the more it will return dividends many times over.

Implementation and Control. How will the business implement and control the marketing and advertising budget, and how will it determine success or failure? In this section explain both the expectations and the implementation.

Timing. How does the timing of the marketing plan and the expenditure of the funds match with the operational plan and follow-though?   (Remember,   luck   =   timing   and preparedness.)

Contingency Planning. Plan for contingencies – the big one being, if this marketing plan fails, what will the business do then? Other contingencies to consider are: What will happen if the market changes?   What if the advertising is not working? What is the second plan to back up the first?

Chapter 5
RESOURCES

For many business plans, this is the most important section. Resources, access to information, permitting, licensing, references and citations should validate the model. While many resources are provided here, it is vital to gain access to industry information through associations as well. (Some are provided as examples below.) Addresses and contact information change from time to time so be sure to check for the latest information. It is also important to check local, municipal, county and state resources. Los Angeles and California are used only as examples here. Go to www.sumatici.com to check out a state by state summary. These sources are in alphabetical order.

We'll start by proving data about the importance of small businesses. How important are small businesses to the U.S. economy? Small firms:
1. Represent 99.7 percent of all employer firms;
2. Employ just over half of all private sector employees;
3. Pay 44 percent of total U.S. private payroll;
4. Have generated 64 percent of net new jobs over the past 15 years;
5. Create more than half of the nonfarm private gross domestic product (GDP);
6. Hire 40 percent of high tech workers (such as scientists, engineers, and computer programmers);
7. Are 52 percent home-based and 2 percent franchises;
8. Made up 97.3 percent of all identified exporters and produced 30.2 percent of the known export value in FY 2007;
9. Produce 13 times more patents per employee than large patenting firms; these patents are twice as likely as large firm patents to be among the one percent most cited.

Sources: (Office of Advocacy's Research and Statistics page) http://www.sba.gov/advocacy/7495/8420: U.S. Dept. of Commerce, Bureau of the Census and International Trade Admin; Advocacy-funded research by Kathryn Kobe, 2007; CHI Research, 2003; U.S. Dept. of Labor, Bureau of Labor Statistics.

The survival rate of businesses is also interesting: Seven out of ten new employer firms last at least two years, and about half survive five years. More specifically, according to new Census data, 69 percent of new employer establishments born to new firms in 2000 survived at least two years, and 51 percent survived five or more years. Firms born in 1990 had very similar survival rates. With most firms starting small, 99.8 percent of the new employer establishments were started by small firms. Survival rates were similar across states and major industries. (Source: U.S Dept. of Commerce, Bureau of the Census, Business Dynamics Statistics. Note that the figures may be skewed by the occurrence of new firms opening multiple establishments in their first few years. (www.sba.gov/advocacy/7495/8430)

An estimated 627,200 new employer firms began operations in 2008, and 595,600 firms closed that year. This amounts to an annual turnover of about 10 percent for entry and 10 percent for exit. Nonemployer firms have turnover rates three times as high as those of employer firms, mostly because of easier entry and exit conditions. (www.sba.gov/advocacy/7495/8423)

BUSINESS RESOURCES

Air Quality Management District (AQMD). The South Coast AQMD believes that all that live or work in this area have a right to breathe clean air. AQMD is committed to undertaking all necessary steps to protect public health from air pollution, with sensitivity to the impacts of its actions on the community and businesses. This is accomplished through a comprehensive program of planning, regulation, compliance assistance, enforcement, monitoring, technology advancement and public education. The AQMD is the air pollution control agency for all of Orange County and the urban portions of Los Angeles, Riverside and San Bernardino counties. Different types and levels of air pollution can cause or contribute to everything from watery eyes and fatigue to respiratory disease, lung damage, cancer, birth defects and premature death. Because this area's smog problem is so severe, AQMD often finds itself at the forefront of the nation's emission reduction efforts. AQMD is responsible for controlling emissions primarily from stationary sources of air pollution. These can include anything from large power plants and refineries to the corner gas station.

Better Business Bureau (BBB). Join the BBB just before opening the business so their information is current and accurate. The BBB will assist with customer questions and disputes, and can provide credibility when potential clients research the business. (Source: www.bbb.org)

Colleges and Universities. Colleges and universities offer job training, host job fairs, job placement services, job posting services and job screening programs. In addition, they can verify a potential employee's certificates, diplomas and other qualifications. Finally, the best research resources in the world are often in the University library. Last, many professors will provide assistance, when asked or as part of a program through the school.

Contractor's State Licensing Board. This board provides information on application and examination requirements, contractor license status, complaint information and law and regulation updates for the construction industry.

County Health Department (DHS). The mission of county health departments is "[t]o ensure access to high-quality, patient-centered, cost-effective health care County residents through direct services at DHS facilities and through collaboration with community and university partners." The DHS also provides training for food handlers and restaurateurs, and conducts health standard inspections for applicable county businesses. Please contact the appropriate county health department for laws, rules and regulations which may apply to business operations in that county.

Employment Development Department (EDD). The Employment Development Department promotes state economic growth by providing services to keep employers, employees, and job seekers competitive. Established in 1936, the EDD provides an economic line of defense against the effects of unemployment – assisting not only the individual, but also the local community.

Federal Trade Commission (FTC). The FTC deals with issues that touch the economic lives of most Americans. In fact, the agency has a long tradition of maintaining a competitive marketplace for both consumers and businesses. Consumers who refer to care labels in their clothes, product warranties or stickers showing the energy costs of home appliances are using information required by the FTC. Businesses must be familiar with the laws requiring truthful advertising or prohibiting price fixing. These laws also are administered by the FTC.

Internal Revenue Service (IRS). The IRS is a bureau of the Department of the Treasury and one of the world's most efficient tax administrators. Its mission is to provide America's taxpayers top quality service by helping them understand and meet their tax responsibilities and by applying the tax law with integrity and fairness to all.

Moody's. Through *Moody's* it's possible to research competitors and vendor information and pull credit reports on potential competitors and/or vendors. *Moody's* does charge a fee for membership or for credit information. (Source: www.moodys.com)

Municipal Resources: City resources typically provide great local, relevant data and assistance in starting and operating a company locally. Cities have a serious incentive to ensure businesses succeed for their tax and job base potential. City departments to investigate include: City manager's office, City business license department; City Planner's office; City Economic Planning & Development Departments; City Libraries; City Redevelopment Agencies; City Economic Development Councils.

National Business Association (NBA). In 1982, the *National Business Association*, a non-profit organization for the self-employed, small business owners, entrepreneurs and professionals, was founded. The NBA continuously strives to provide its members with vital support programs, cost and time saving products and services in the areas of business, lifestyle, education and health. (www.nationalbusiness.org)

Regional Occupational Programs (ROP). The *Regional Occupational Program* is a public education service that provides practical, hands-on career preparation and career guidance. The ROP is designed to provide students with the technical skills required for particular jobs. Community-based internships in local business and industry sites are offered in many classes. Every course offers a unit on employment seeking skills, which includes job application, resume and interview preparation. Their website is www.esgvrop.org.

Secretary of State. Through a states Secretary of State website, research can be done for all public company data; verify corporation filing status; conduct business name searches; and conduct industry requirements governed by the Secretary of State. In most states, the information provided free of charge.

Service Corps of Retired Executives (SCORE). SCORE offers, at no charge, two types of confidential counseling to help and entrepreneur get started in business or improve an existing one. SCORE offers confidential face-to-face counseling at no charge to U. S. citizens. Most counseling sessions are conducted at a SCORE location. However, on-site counseling is available when a more complete evaluation of an on-going business is needed.

Securities and Exchange Commission (SEC). The mission of the U.S. Securities and Exchange Commission is to protect investors, maintain fair, orderly, and efficient markets and facilitate capital formation. The laws and rules that govern the securities industry in the United States derive from a simple and straightforward concept: all investors, whether large institutions or private individuals, should have access to certain basic facts about an investment prior to buying it, and so long as they hold it. To achieve this, the SEC requires public companies to disclose meaningful financial and other information to the public. This provides a common pool of knowledge for all investors to use to judge for themselves whether to buy, sell, or hold a particular security. (www.sec.gov)

Small Business Development Centers (SBDC). The SBDC provides multiple programs and is usually in business to support businesses by providing resources and access to capital. Most centers work with banks and other lenders to supplement loan applications. Many also provide business owners and operators with the management, marketing and financial skills necessary for their companies to survive and flourish in today's challenging business environment. For example, the *Southeast Los Angeles Small Business Development Center* is a non-profit agency dedicated to providing resources, knowledge and technical assistance to help the seasoned business owners and/or entrepreneurs succeed in today's challenging business environment.

State Board of Equalization. The mission of the State Board of Equalization is to serve the public through fair, effective and efficient tax administration. Created in California in 1879 by a constitutional amendment, the Board of Equalization was initially charged with responsibility for ensuring that county property tax assessment practices were equal and uniform throughout the state. Currently the tax programs administered by the Board are concentrated in four general areas: sales and use taxes, property taxes, special taxes and the tax appellate program. (www.boe.ca.gov) Please be sure to contact your own state's Board of Equalization or similar state governing body regarding business taxes.

United National Global Compact. The UN Global Compact is a strategic policy initiative for businesses that are committed to aligning their operations and strategies with ten universally accepted principles in the areas of human rights, labor, environment and anti-corruption. By doing so, business, as a primary driver of globalization, can help ensure that markets, commerce, technology and finance advance in ways that benefit economies and societies everywhere. The website offers hundreds of business association resources. (Unglobalcompact.org)

U.S. Bureau of Labor & Statistics. Per their mission: "The Bureau of Labor Statistics of the U.S. Department of Labor is the principal Federal agency responsible for measuring labor market activity, working conditions, and price changes in the economy." (www.bls.gov)

U.S. Census Bureau. The mission of the US Census bureau is, "...[we] serves as the leading source of quality data about the nation's people and economy. We honor privacy, protect confidentiality, share our expertise globally, and conduct our work openly. We are guided on this mission by our strong and capable workforce, our readiness to innovate, and our abiding commitment to our customers." (www.census.org)

U.S. Chamber of Commerce. The U.S. Chamber of Commerce is the world's largest business federation representing the interests of more than three million businesses of all sizes, sectors and regions, as well as state and local chambers and industry associations. More than 96% of U.S. Chamber members are small businesses with 100 employees or fewer. (www.uschamber.com)

U.S. Department of Commerce. The historic mission of the Department is "to foster, promote, and develop the foreign and domestic commerce" of the United States. This has evolved, as a result of legislative and administrative additions, to encompass broadly the responsibility to foster, serve, and promote the nation's economic development and technological advancement. (www.commerce.gov.)

U.S. Immigration and Naturalization Service (INS). The INS requires that all hired staff complete *Form I-9, Employment Eligibility Verification.* Those completing the form must show specified documentation to confirm their eligibility to live and work in the U.S. There is recorded information that reviews relevant topics of interest. (www.uscis.gov)

U.S. Small Business Administration (SBA). The U.S. Small Business Administration was created in 1953 as an independent agency of the federal government to aid, counsel, assist and protect the interests of small business concerns, to preserve free competitive enterprise and to maintain and strengthen the overall economy of our nation. Although the SBA has grown and evolved in the years since it was established in 1953, the bottom line mission remains the same. The SBA helps Americans start, build and grow businesses. (www.sba.gov)

Utility Companies. Southern California Edison's (SCE) well-being is directly linked to the economic vitality of its customer base. As the business community prospers, so does the community at large. This is why SCE supports economic and business development efforts to retain, expand and attract business and to increase the competitiveness of its business customers. SCE's Economic and Business Development (E&BD) group offers guidance, resources, and assistance to business customers to help them make informed decisions and to help increase their competitiveness. Many public utility companies offer extensive assistance to business owners. Locate and inquire at the public utility companies in the district where your business will operate.

Websites: When conducting industry research, remember that some websites charge fees while others do not. Some of the information gathered on these sites can be invaluable in conducting research about competitors and potential vendors. Among the hundreds of websites for industry research these are the most utilized:

www.onesource.com
www.firstgov.gov
www.allbusiness.com
www.business.gov
www.smartbiz.com
www.hoovers.com
www.Marketresearch.com

SERVING YOUR COMMUNITY

An entrepreneur might not think about the Kiwanis, Rotary Club, Lions Club, chambers of commerce, business-to-business referral groups, supporting (or joining) a non-profit or attending church as part of his business. But if a business owner ignores these, he's missing an opportunity to learn and serve.

There is an old saying, "Work where you live and live where you work." For a business owner, this is true on more than one level. First, an entrepreneur is not just a member of the community where he resides. As a business owner, he provides jobs for other members of the community. On another level, think of the opportunities for business when the business owner of *that* business is seen directly involved in the community through service organizations, business referral groups, non-profits and churches. Integrity and character of the owner are seen by the entire community.

A lot of business is done on the basis of relationships. For example, when someone knows a computer repairman and his home computer breaks down, does he run to the Yellow Pages or does he call the repairman he knows? Unless the repairman he *knows* is a total dud (and he'd know that only if he did business with him before or heard something negative from someone he trusted), he will call the repairman he knows. He isn't going to ask if the repairman is the cheapest. He isn't going to ask if he's the best. He *knows* him and he trusts that repairman to fix his computer.

The point is, by becoming involved with service organizations, business referral groups, non-profits and churches a business owner gives himself (and by proxy his business) more positive exposure in the community. And not only that, he'll be doing some additional good for the community too!

QUOTES FOR ENTREPRENEURS

"Happiness is when what you think, what you say, and what you do are in harmony."

- Mahatma Gandhi

◆

"Shared joy is a double joy; shared sorrow is half sorrow."

- Swedish proverb

◆

"God is the brave man's hope, and not the coward's excuse."

- Plutarch

◆

"It is easy to be brave from a safe distance."

- Aesop

◆

"Who bravely dares must sometimes risk a fall."

- Tobias Smollett

◆

"Courage is the ladder on which all the other virtues mount."

- Clare Booth Luce

◆

"Time is the only commodity that is on an even playing field with everyone regardless of financial status, race, color, religion or creed."

-Anonymous

◆

"Happiness could be defined as the emotion of progress toward desirable goals. There is an instant of contemplation of the last goal in which one is content. But contentment becomes boredom immediately that new goals do not come to view. There is no unhappy thing than a man who has accomplished all his ends in life."

-L. Ron Hubbard

♦

"You cannot help the poor by destroying the rich."

- Lincoln

♦

"You cannot strengthen the weak by weakening the strong."

- Lincoln

♦

"You cannot lift the wage earner up by pulling the wage payer down."

- Lincoln

♦

"If we ever forget that we're one nation under God, then we will be a nation gone under."

- Ronald Reagan

♦

"Inches make champions."

-Vince Lombardi

♦

"Well done is better than well said."

- B. Franklin

♦

"Do first things first and second things not at all."
                                        - Peter Drucker

                    ♦

"The journey of a thousand miles must begin with a single step."
                                        - Lao Tzu

                    ♦

"Water and words... Easy to pour impossible to recover."
                                        -Chinese Proverb

                    ♦

"Do not speak - unless it improves on silence."
                                        -Buddhist Saying

                    ♦

"We cannot see our reflection in running water. It is only in still water that we can see."
                                        -Taoist Proverb

                    ♦

Student says "I am very discouraged. What should I do?"
Master says, "Encourage others."
                                        - Zen Proverb

                    ♦

"When the pupil is ready to learn, a teacher will appear."
                                        - Zen Proverb

                    ♦

"It takes a wise man to learn from his mistakes, but an even wiser man to learn from others."
                                        - Zen Proverb

                    ♦

"When the character of a man is not clear to you, look at his friends."

- Japanese Proverb

♦

"To know the road ahead, ask those coming back."

- Chinese Proverb

♦

"Give a man a fish and you feed him for a day. Teach a man to fish and you feed him for a lifetime."

- Chinese Proverb

♦

"Although gold dust is precious, when it gets in your eyes, it obstructs your vision."

- Hsi-Tang

♦

"Try not to become a man of success, but rather try to become a man of value."

- Albert Einstein

RECOMMENED BOOKS

A Purpose Driven Life	Rick Warren
Art of Happiness	Dalai Lama & Howard C. Cutler, M.D.
Art of War	Sun Tzu
As a Man Thinketh	James Allen
Awaken the Giant Within	Anthony Robbins
Bible	Old & New Testament

Blink: The Power of Thinking Without Thinking
Malcolm Gladwell

Good to Great	Jim Collins

How to Master the Art of Selling Anything
Tom Hopkins

How to Stop Worrying and Start Living
Dale Carnegie

How to Win Friends & Influence People
Dale Carnegie

Live your dreams	Les Brown

Outliers: The Story of Success
Malcolm Gladwell

Rich Dad, Poor Dad	Robert T. Kiyosaki

Seven Habits of Highly Affected People
Stephen Covey

Seven Strategies for Wealth and Happiness
Jim Rohn

Something to Smile about   Zig Ziglar

The Greatest Miracle in the World
Og Mandino

The Greatest Salesman in the World
Og Mandino

The Greatest Secret in the World
Og Mandino

The Millionaire Mind   Thomas J. Stanley

The Millionaire Next Door   Thomas J. Stanley

The Power of Positive Thinking
Norman Vincent Peale

The Richest Man in Babylon   George S. Clason

The Road Less Traveled   Scott Peck

The Tipping Point: How Little Things Make a Big Difference
Malcolm Gladwell

Think and Grow Rich   Napoleon Hill

[Glossary will be added in final print version.]

[Index will be added in final print version.]

Tony Drexel Smith's goal is to serve entrepreneurs seeking incubator services, capital and business finance documents including professional-grade business plans, memorandums, credit application presentations as well as accounting and tax services.

These deliverables support access to capital with investment bankers, venture capitalists, angel investors and commercial lenders. Tony defines success as serving clients with ethical and honest work on a "best-efforts" basis while also maintaining strict adherence to regulatory compliance.

Tony wrote or supervised the production of hundreds of business finance documents since 1995. He has reviewed more than 1,400 business plans and been a strategic management consultant to more than 285 clients in dozens of industries, sectors and sub-sectors. Smith has had a direct or indirect role in developing more than 700 business plans. He has managed up to 450 employees, independent contractors or teams in retail sales environments.

Tony is a graduate of the University of La Verne with a B.A. in Business Administration; Cum Laude Honors.

Tony is a Veteran of Foreign Wars – United States Marine Corps from 1988 to 1993. He is married to Leslye Galati-Smith – together they have six children.

Darrel Whitehead serves as the Executive Director of Darrel Whitehead CPAs, an accounting practice that grosses $1,300,000 in revenues and performs tax, accounting, and administrative services. The Firm is currently serving more than 600 clients and maintains competitive differentiation by supporting business finance, IT and platform accounting solutions for internet businesses. Beginning his career at Arthur Andersen, Darrel moved on to a regional CPA Firm, Singer Lewak in business management developing expertise in taxation and managing the business affairs of high profile clients in the music and entertainment industries. Darrel divides his time between his two residences in Huntington Beach, California and Cortez, Colorado. He is a private pilot and avid golfer.

TECHNICAL EXPERIENCE:

Litigation support
Business valuation, controllable cash testimony (Divorce).

Taxation
Personally managed over 300 tax audits. Overall responsibility for the firms tax policies;
Develops business and tax strategies.

Merger/Acquisitions
Personally supported and supervised 15 client business sales.

Audit Supervision
Managed over 200 certified audits in the law, medical, employee benefit, and professional services industries.

CERTIFICATIONS
Certified Public Accountant in California; Member CAL CPA Society; Member AICPA.